Parents: Give Your Kid A Chance

Ken Poure

with

Dave Stoop

Harvest House Publishers
Irvine, California 92714

PARENTS: GIVE YOUR KID A CHANCE

Copyright © 1977 Harvest House Publishers
Irvine, California 92714
Library of Congress Catalog
Card Number: 77-82035
ISBN 0-89081-068-0

Printed in the United States of America

This book is dedicated to

Melba,

my high school sweetheart

my wonderful wife

the mother of our children,

Sandra, David and Mark

who made this book a reality

Ken Poure

Contents

Chapter

1

ON FLYING
A KITE

Raising kids is like flying a kite. Only those who are too young to try, or too old to remember, believe it's a simple task. The rest of us know what a difficult job it really is. We only *act* like it's a snap.

The kite-flying authorities (whoever they are) are all in agreement that the early steps are the most crucial. One expert said, "Give me a kite in its early stages and I will determine its future!" When pressed for the meaning of his words, he went on to describe how every step in the early building process is important. The frame must be constructed from carefully selected wood. When finished, it must be strong, yet light-weight. Equally important is the precise way the paper is attached to the frame.

Then with a fervor characteristic of every expert, he went on to explain the importance of the tail. Often considered a last minute addition, the tail is really of the highest importance. The proper material must be selected based on the wind conditions, and cut to the exact length. Then the necessary knots are tied prior to attaching the tail to the kite.

Both parents and kite-flyers know the importance of these early stages. We go to great pains to make sure that all the ingredients for success are present. We carefully avoid as many pitfalls as possible, knowing there is always the potential of a kite-eating tree or high-voltage wires lurking nearby. But the time always comes when, with a mixture of fear and courage, we must launch our masterpiece into the cold and dangerous environment.

Now, all the foundation work is supposed to pay off. If we did a good job in the early steps, the rest should be easy. But the winds can change. Our calculations on the length of the tail can be off, and our kite either spins wildly out of control or sinks heavily to the ground. With kites, but not with kids, we go back to the drawing room.

Let's assume that all our preparations are correct and our kite takes to the sky like an eagle. This "letting go" time is the real test of the skill of every kite-flyer. For the magical difference between the kite that barely gets off the ground and the one that scrapes the clouds is the way we release the string. We've got to keep just the right tension on the line.

Just like raising kids!

You can do a bang-up job with your kids during those crucial early years. You can do all the "right" things, like help coach your son or daughter's Little League team, be a room mother, etc., but when the time comes for them to start flying on their own—the teen years—all kinds of problems and heartaches develop. It's a painful experience to let your kids go into the adult world today. There are just too many potential dangers lurking at every corner.

But launch them, you must. The question is how do you hold the string during these years? If a parent holds the string too tight, there is the danger that their kids will spin out of control, get themselves tangled in a kite-eating tree, or crash. On the other hand, if a parent tries to keep the tension on the string too taut, everything and everyone is under tremendous strain. Without warning, the whole kite can break apart, or the string will snap and the kite will be lost forever.

I've talked with many parents who have done both. Some jerked on the string and watched it break. With tears, they tell me how they haven't heard from one of their kids for years, except through another person. Others tell me how they let the string go slack, or even put it down, only to watch their kids spin crazily out of control. In each situation, the pain has been intense.

But you say your problems with your kids are not that serious—yet? And it still hurts? I know it does, because all of our problems are relative. When you are the one experiencing the pain, it hurts! The parent, whose adolescent is trying to catch a new strong wind that's heading in the wrong direction, hurts just as much as the parent of the young teen who has just broken the string. In each situation, the parent struggles intensely with feelings of failure and despair. This is often complicated by a sense of aloneness—no one else has experienced the problems we face and failed like we have failed.

Well, maybe you did make some mistakes. But then, every parent does, simply because parents are human. And humans still are not perfect! Many times, outside factors break the string. In these cases, the parents have no control over the circumstances, and the problems are not a reflection on their abilities as parents. The influence of drugs, music, and peers are all strong winds that can suddenly change direction, producing a real nose dive. In these situations, all a parent can do is hope, pray and love.

Sound hopeless? It isn't! Studies have shown that often the child who struggles the hardest ends up flying the highest. The secret seems to be in the way the parents hang on to the string.

This book is about giving your kids a chance to really fly in life. We talk about the family a bit, and about the early foundation years. But we also talk about how to hang on to the string. Perhaps the best place to begin is to check out the owner's manual.

To Think About:
1. What other ways can you think of to describe the process of raising children, besides kite-flying?
2. What part of parenting do you fear the most? Why? What part does your spouse fear the most? Why? Talk together about your answers.
3. What part of parenting do you enjoy the most? Why? What part does your spouse enjoy the most? Why? Talk together about your answers.

Chapter

2

CHECK THE OWNER'S MANUAL

Check The
Owner's Manual

I am convinced that the greatest happiness you and I can experience on this planet is available behind the front doors of our homes. Real joy is found in human relationship. And the most fulfilling relationships we can experience are found within our family. The pursuit of happiness takes us on many tangents, but the real pleasures in life are found with those we love the most.

If our family relationship can be the most rewarding, it can also be the most destructive. For behind those doors, we also meet our greatest challenge. We need all the help we can get.

When I was first married, I was in the used car business. I was known as the world's smallest high-volume dealer. Every time I bought a car for resale, one of the first things I would do was check the glove compartment for an owner's manual. And whenever I found one, I would think to myself, "Ooh, Kenny, you've got a nice one here! The previous owner really cared about this car."

Obviously I didn't need that owner's manual to sell the car. And whoever bought the car didn't need the manual in order to own or drive the car.

I remember a particular car I owned some time ago. It was back in those days when only a few people were affluent enough to afford air conditioning. I was always bothered with that car, thinking there had to be some ventilation down by the feet. I looked all over that car and never did find any air vents. Several years later, I had a car just like that one on my lot, only this one had an owner's manual in the glove compartment. And while leafing through that manual I finally discovered where the manufacturer had hidden those crazy vents.

You see, I found out by experience that reading the manual helped me discover some things I would never have known. Agreed, the owner's manual isn't required reading, but the person who is interested in knowing all the capabilities of the car will take the time to read that important booklet.

If you are interested in successfully meeting the challenge of developing your children so they can enjoy life in all its fullness, let me suggest that you begin by checking out the owner's manual—the Bible. Of course you don't need to read the Bible in order to survive on planet earth. You really don't even need to own one. But there are going to be a lot of things happening in your family with those you love that you will never understand if you do not check the Bible. For, like the owner's manual in a new car, the Bible tells you what your Creator intended for you to know so that you can enjoy life. It's in the pages of the Bible that you discover what Jesus meant when He said, "My purpose is to give life in all its fullness."

I find all kinds of help in the Bible. There are important principles that I can use to enrich my own life. And there are principles that I can use as a parent to give my kids a better chance to become all they can and want to be. Basic to my attitude towards these principles is my faith in the author. That's why I think some of the most important words are found right on the first page: "In the beginning God created . . . ." Your attitude toward these five words will determine your attitude toward all the other principles that follow. Here's why I believe that's true.

If you take a lazy attitude toward your faith and trust in God, that attitude will lead you to a rather shabby commitment to the other principles. Likewise, if your faith is strong and solid, your commitment will be firm and practical.

The way I see it, either these first five words in Genesis are true, or they are false. But how can we know? We weren't there in the beginning. Let's check out the options. Suppose we say, "These words are false." Where does that leave us? One possible solution is to say that the universe is the result of cosmic chance. But how do we know that? Only by faith! So even the atheist lives by faith. He doesn't *know* there is no God, he only *believes* there is no God.

The big problem I have with this point of view is the fact that if you start with impersonal matter, such as gases, electrons, or some kind of impulses, where does personality come from? Can personality come from non-personality? Can non-intelligence lead to intelligence? Oh, to believe that takes gobs of faith! Whenever I meet someone who believes these ideas, I say, "Congratulations! You have more faith than I have!" And they'll respond with, "What do you mean?" "Well," I tell them, "if you don't believe in a personal creator or in God, then you have to believe in equations like this: Nobody + Nothing = Everything! Don't tell me that doesn't take faith."

Personally, I would rather place my faith in the truth of those five important words. I want to affirm that God was in the beginning. We all came from something, and the something is personal—it is God! I can say with confidence that God exists. He is real and He is active in my life today.

If you can accept that basic concept, we can start building a launching pad for our discussion of the relationships that exist within the family. Having affirmed that God is and that He is active, we can look at some of the principles he has given us in the Bible—the owner's manual.

One of the first things we find is that when God made you and me He made us in His image. That's fantastic when you stop and think about what that means. He made each of us like Him! Every human being carries within himself the qualities of God. That explains why we are creative, why we have personality, why we can love and desire to have companionship. Because we are made like God, we have the ability to think and to reason. All of these characteristics, and many more, are present within us because we are created in the image of God. Every member of your family, including your children, is made in the likeness of God.

We also discover as we look through the owner's manual that at a point in time God said, "It isn't good for man to be alone." Companion-ship is a high priority. God wants us to enjoy relationships.

For many years, our society has interpreted that to mean marriage. When a person hits his twenties and he's not married, we have our subtle little jokes: "What's wrong? Need to change your deodorant?" Or if we see him with the same person more than once, we ask, "Set the date yet?" You know how it goes. These things are said in fun, but they create a lot of pressure at the same time.

Fortunately, we are recognizing that there

can be a lot of neat relationships that don't involve marriage. But it is still true that the deepest form of companionship, which includes not only the psychological and sociological but the biological part of us as well, can only be found in the context of marriage. God created marriage to satisfy our deepest needs. And God still considers this to be the basic relationship in our human experiences.

The principle that best describes the marriage relationship is that a man shall *leave* his mother and father and *cleave* unto his own wife. These are interesting words that I am sure you have heard many times at weddings. But do you realize that many of the problems that arise in marriages are rooted in either not leaving or not cleaving.

Some people get married but never leave the emotional ties they have with their parents. They refuse to grow up. I am sure you have seen this in some people, for the problem of not leaving is easy to identify. But how does one cleave?

Cleaving does not mean that I cling to my wife or never let her leave my sight. No, I think of cleaving as a more emotional idea. Some practical ways that I cleave to my wife simply involve "promoting" her. For example, if I'm with a bunch of guys, and one of them tells some weird story that puts down the idea of marriage or belittles the wife, I say something like, "Hey man, I might buy that bag if my wife weren't so sweet. But wow, she satisfies my deepest needs.

Really!" I drop that little baby into the conversation and it really shakes some of them up, because they have not yet learned how to be positive cleavers.

Another aspect of cleaving is found in the rest of that verse: "A man shall leave his father and mother and cleave unto his wife, *and the two shall become one flesh.*" Cleaving involves the physical aspect of the man/woman relationship.

How long is that supposed to last? We probably had over 24,000 kids come to our camp program last year, and it's amazing how many of them just couldn't handle the idea of me walking around the campground with my arm around my wife, stealing a kiss every now and then. Someone my age is supposed to have outgrown the desire for any physical relationship with his wife.

Some of these kids are in high school and don't realize their parents know anything about sex! I say to them, "Now wait a minute. How do you think you got here—the stork?" That starts them thinking again. They are surprised to discover that God has designed the love relationship to grow right on through the years. You don't die at thirty! You keep right on way beyond that. We had a guy at camp who was 82 years old. I asked him how long you're sexually alive and he replied, "You'd better ask somebody older than me!" Isn't that great! I sure think it is. God has a fantastic plan that includes cleaving to our spouse. That's a foundation principle.

We need to draw one more important principle out of our owner's manual. If we want to really give our kids a chance in life, we need to know the will of God for our family. And we can. In Ephesians 5:17 and 18 KJV, Paul says, "Wherefore, be ye not unwise, but understanding what the will of the Lord is. And, be not drunk with wine . . . but be filled with the Spirit!"

There it is—God's will for the family. But you have a choice. You can be a Christian and not be controlled by the Spirit; that's your choice. But understand this, God's will is for each of us and for our families to be filled with His Spirit.

The word "filled" is an ambiguous word. One of the songs we sing talks about our lives as cups which God is going to fill. What does He fill us with? How full is full? When I checked out the way that word was used when Paul wrote this letter, I discovered that it is a military term that means "to be under the authority of . . . ." Let's substitute that phrase and see what we get: "Be under the authority of the Spirit."

When I say that, I can understand what Paul means. It's kind of like getting a job. When I am offered a job, I am told how much I will be paid and that I am expected to arrive at eight o'clock in the morning prepared to put in eight hours of work for five days each week. Now watch this—when I report for work the next morning at eight o'clock sharp and walk through the door, I am saying to my employer that for the next eight hours, "Not my will, but thine be done." I place myself under his authority.

The mechanics of being filled by the Spirit are the same as renting my body and abilities to an employer for eight hours a day. In both cases I am placing myself under someone else's authority.

Another way to look at this is to consider the body itself. My body has many parts and I'm up here someplace in the head. I have control over my body. My hand is under the authority of the head—of me. Now what do I expect of my hand when I say it is under my authority? What would you think if one morning you woke up and your hand was running all over the place, bouncing around? You say to your hand, "What are you doing, hand?" And your hand replies, "Well, I woke up before you did and I've been doing my own thing. My four fingers and my thumb got together and had a committee meeting and decided what to do today. I'll check back in with you if I get in trouble." Would you want a hand like that? Not me! I want my hand to be present and reporting for duty.

I use two phrases to describe what I mean when I say that something is under the authority of something else. The first phrase is *restfully available*. A few minutes ago, my hand was resting on my leg. Do you know what it was doing? Nothing! And my hand was in the center of my will. Some people have the mistaken idea that to be under the authority of God's Spirit is to be constantly active. Not true! You don't have to be doing something to be under the authority of your heavenly Father. Just be restfully available.

What could your hand be doing right now? Let's put a little personality into your hand while it's holding onto this book. Suppose your hand got to thinking and decided that holding a book was a rather mundane task. There are more important things to be done. And so your hand starts worrying about all the other things it should be doing. Then it starts to worry about how soon it will have to turn a page. And before too long, your hand has worked itself into a lather with worry, worry and more worry. But no, that's not what's happening. Your hand is very content with its task and it is restfully available, ready to turn the page.

The other phrase is *instantly obedient*. When I decide that I want my hand to do something, I want it to be instantly obedient. I don't want an argument, I want action. "Scratch my nose." I want it done now, not five minutes later. And if my hand were not restfully available and instantly obedient, I'd be on my way to visit the doctor to find out what's wrong.

Very practically, that's what it means to be filled with God's Holy Spirit. I am filled when I am willingly under the authority of God's Spirit. And that occurs when I am restfully available to what God wants me to do and instantly obedient to His every request. This is experienced in the family as the parents place themselves under the authority of God's Spirit and then encourage each child to make that same choice. This is

God's will for each of us and for our family.

There's much more to discover in the owner's manual. As we fit each piece together to form a solid foundation, the mortar that holds it all together is the source of our faith. If our faith is based on the reality of a dynamic, living God, then we will be willing to accept His principles for living and actively seek practical ways we can use them each day.

To think about:

1. With whom do you share your deepest friendship?
2. Can you say that your spouse is also one of your closest friends? Would the other members of your family agree?
3. How was your day today? Can you describe times when you were under the authority of the Holy Spirit? Can you describe times when you chose not to be under His authority? What made the difference in your choices?
4. How would you describe your family? Are family decisions based on the principle of being filled with the Spirit? How do the other members of your family feel about this?

Chapter
3

THREE CHEERS
FOR THE
DIFFERENCES

Three Cheers
For The Differences

Why did I ever marry her (or him)? Did you ever ask yourself that question? Wow, Melba and I sure did! We were only eighteen years old when we got married. We were still kids! And did we ever have a rough time. We almost gave up after two years. But for some reason, we hung in there. We were such opposites—and still are. And when I quit the used-car business and started working in a Christian Camp ministry, things got even tougher.

In the midst of our struggles we found hope. One day a big manila folder arrived in the mail. I opened it to find a book manuscript and a letter from my pastor-friend, Tim LaHaye. He wondered if Melba and I would check over his manuscript and make any suggestions before he sent it off to the publisher.

Well, the only time we could read was in bed at night. We agreed we would do it together; so the first evening we jumped in bed and started reading. It was really funny. As we were reading along, suddenly Melba started chuckling to herself and nodding her head in agreement. A couple of pages later I found myself doing the same thing. We kept on reading long into the wee hours of the morning. The more we read, the more we understood what we really had been struggling with for over sixteen years. It was the most revealing thing that had happened to us in our marriage.

I want to share some of this with you because, unless you and your spouse are pulling in the same direction, your kids are going to have only half the chance they could have if you're both heading the same way.

One of the things we discovered was that opposites are attracted to each other. Now you and I have heard that all our lives, but have you ever stopped to figure out why that's true? I finally did. One reason is that each of us knows our weak areas and is usually attracted to someone who is strong where we are weak. You've noticed how the organized guy is often attracted to a wheezy girl. Intellectuals tend to have dum-dums for a spouse. Not always, I agree, but the tendency is certainly there for people to choose a partner that exemplifies everything they wish they were.

That sure was true of Melba and me. I

remember the first time I saw her way back in junior high school. My first impression was how neatly she dressed—everyday a little pleated skirt, neatly polished saddle oxfords, bobby socks, hair all combed up in a pompadour, every curl in place. Remember back in the forties? Everyday she was just immaculate.

And here I was—super-gross. The big thing for the guys was to wear one pair of cords for the whole semester. And if you could get them dirty enough, they would stand up in the corner all by themselves. I think I succeeded every semester. I was a disaster in every area that required any organization. And was I ever attracted to that little bundle of organized energy. After we got married, she told me she was attracted to my free-wheeling style and hang-loose attitude. What she admired in me was my ability to talk to anyone. I had even talked my way into being elected president of the student body. Whereas Melba was timid and quiet around other people. We both saw qualities in each other that we desired for ourselves; so we got married.

Great, huh? Two opposites become one; so now we are complete. No way! Just the opposite happened. When we got married her secret ambition was to organize me. And I resisted to the point of even trying to disorganize her. In the process, I discovered a new law, the "law of repulsion." Whatever one spouse does to extreme, the other spouse will do to the opposite extreme. If the husband is the last of the big spenders, his wife will become a female scrooge. But if the husband suddenly changes and begins to tighten up his spending habits, the wife will go on a shopping spree. We played this see-saw game for years, until we discovered a way to turn it all around and started to build on each other's strengths. And it all began that night we were reading together in bed.

We discovered that everyone has inherited a basic temperament. According to this theory, which has been traced all the way back to the brilliant Greek physician and philosopher, Hippocrates, there are four basic tempera-ments. Two are extroverts and two are introverts. What often happens in marriage is that the introverts and the extroverts are attracted to each other. Let's look first at each of the temperaments and consider how they affect our relationship with our spouse. In the next chapter we will look at how these temperaments affect our children and our relationship with them.

Melancholy

SOME POSITIVE CHARACTERISTICS	SOME HANG-UPS
Gifted	Moody
Analytical	Negative
Sensitive	Rigid
Artistic	Self-centered
Perfectionist	Touchy
Conscientious	Revengeful
Aesthetic	Theoretical
Musical	Impractical
Idealistic	Persecution-prone
Loyal	Unsociable
Self-sacrificing	Critical
Self-disciplined	

The first temperament is an introvert—the Melancholic temperament. This is Melvin and Marilee Melancholy. Look carefully at their faces. Can you see that they are introverts?

Now these people are very beautiful. They make wonderful artists, musicians, inventors, philosophers and professors. Because they are basically introverted, they enjoy being by themselves and living inside of their own heads. They could spend a month in their room and forget there was even a world going on outside.

Since these gifted, perfectionistic people tend to be analytical and sensitive they are quite discerning. But they can be hard to live with. If your wife is melancholic, you know better than to call her at four o'clock in the afternoon to announce, "Hey, I'm bringing several guests home for dinner. We'll be there in an hour." You know she needs at least a week's warning!

Melancholics have some other hang-ups as well. They can be very moody. This follows naturally from their ability to sink into themselves and be introspective. If this tendency is carried too far or for too long a time, it can lead to severe depression. Melvin and Marilee can get *so* depressed and negative that an observer is sure they will never get over it or change.

And, oh, can they ever be revengeful. They can nurse a grudge for months, even years. They can also be very critical of others. The funny thing is they are often correct in their criticism because they have been thinking about it for weeks.

Phlegmatic

SOME POSITIVE CHARACTERISTICS	SOME HANG-UPS
Calm	Indolent
Quiet	Blase
Easy-going	Unmotivated
Dependable	Spectator
Efficient	Self-protective
Conservative	Selfish
Organized	Stingy
Objective	Indecisive
Practical	Fearful
Leader	Tease
Likeable	
Diplomatic	
Humorous	

Our second temperament is also an introvert, but a happy one. Meet Phil and Phyllis Phlegmatic. They're neat people. You find phlegmatics often make wonderful diplomats, accountants, teachers and technicians. Their calm and quiet disposition runs along on a smooth track. Every time you meet them they seem the same. Nothing gets them riled up. Tell Phil the world is coming to an end and he might say, "Oh?" Or tell Phyllis her house is burning down, and she'll respond with a yawn, "Guess we'll just have to get out."

They are easy-going, usually very dependable, efficient, conservative, well-organized, objective, likeable and diplomatic. They possess a great sense of humor, the dry, subtle kind. If Phil tells a joke, you might not even know it was a joke until several hours later.

Phlegmatics also have weaknesses. They are not morning people. They need at least six cups of coffee to even start to percolate. And they are quite blase about what's going on around them. As a result, they are usually spectators, not participants. If they rise to a position of leadership and someone presents them with an idea, they are likely to say, "Oh, that's a good idea. Why don't you go ahead and do it?"

There is a strong tendency for these people to be stingy and selfish. A favorite question of phlegmatics is "How much will it cost me?" And when they are faced with a decision, be prepared to wait. Shopping with phlegmatics can be plain misery. They'll look at all the shirts, or all the dresses, and then go back through the pile as they agonize over their choice.

Well, these are the two introverts. You'll notice that each has some pluses and some minuses. You may also be thinking that some of these hang-ups are common to all of us. That's true, but the negative aspects of each temperament seem to hold a special power in their life, and the result is basic weaknesses in character that must be tempered.

Choleric

SOME POSITIVE CHARACTERISTICS	SOME HANG-UPS
Strong-willed	Crafty
Determined	Unemotional
Independent	Self-sufficient
Visionary	Unsympathetic
Optimistic	Impetuous
Practical	Proud
Productive	Domineering
Decisive	Inconsiderate
Courageous	Unappreciative
Leader	Unforgiving
Confident	Sarcastic
	Angry-Cruel

Let's meet the extroverts. Here are Charlene and Charlie Choleric. Can you tell what they are like by looking at their faces? These are the people who make the world go 'round. They are the producers, builders, leaders, policemen, hard-nosed executives and the General Pattons of today. The melancholic might design the bridges, but it's the cholerics who see that they are built.

Look at some of their tremendous positive characteristics: strong-willed, determined, independent, visionary—see how the words explode with energy? The men and women who are predominantly choleric always make their presence felt.

But if their positive characteristics are dynamic, their hang-ups can be just as volatile. They are manipulators of the first order. If they don't succeed on the first attempt, they'll play their con-game until they do. And they will *not* give up until they get what they want.

Cholerics have a difficult time showing their emotions. This doesn't mean they are emotionless, only that they just do not know how or why they should express their feelings. "Why do you want me to tell you I love you?" says the choleric spouse. "I told you twenty years ago, and I still feel the same way." Oh, it's so hard to get them even to say, "I love you." My wife has a lot of choleric in her and I get an "I love you" out of her heart maybe three or four times a year. But when I do, wow, she really means it!

And can they ever be tough, impetuous and

unappreciative. Come home with a new hairdo and a choleric husband can just blow you apart: "Well, what happened to you? Run through a steam room? Ha, ha, ha!" And what a memory they have! You get into an argument and they will say, "You always say things like that! I remember what you said four years ago!" I can't even remember what I said yesterday, but the choleric can remember way back. But obviously, since I'm married to one, I've got to admit they are great people!

Sanguine

SOME POSITIVE CHARACTERISTICS	SOME HANG-UPS
Outgoing	Emotional
Personable	Disorganized
Responsive	Undisciplined
Carefree	Restless
Compassionate	Unproductive
Friendly	Weak-willed
Warm	Loud
Talkative	Egocentric
Enthusiastic	Undependable
Likes to please	Exaggerates
	Temper
	Indecisive

Sally and Sam Sanguine represent the last of the four temperaments. They're also extroverts; it's written all over them. See that smile? You can call that their trademark. They are so outgoing, personable, carefree, warm and enthusiastic that you wonder if they are aware of what is going on in the world around them. How can they be on top all of the time?

Since they are almost all mouth, they make excellent sales persons, public speakers, and politicians. And because they are so expressive about everything, they make great actors and actresses. They love to be with people and never seem to lack friends.

I have a lot of sanguine in me and I guess that's why I enjoyed being in the used-car business and now enjoy spending so much time speaking at camp and in family seminars. I love to be with people. I like being in front of a group because it gives me an excuse for talking. If I'm in a crowd, you can always find me by homing in on my constant chatter. My vocal chords are subject to constant exercise!

Rather reluctantly, I must admit that we sanguines also have our hang-ups. I've already described to you how disorganized I am. This is closely related to the tendency to be undisciplined and weak-willed. It's so much easier just to respond to a situation than to make all the effort required to plan ahead. Of course, that creates some complicated difficulties many times. But we're good at "shooting from the hip" when the going gets tough.

Now the understanding of the basic differences in each of these temperaments literally knocked Melba and me out of our bed. We finally understood that our differences are not a threat to each other, they are a normal part of us. And they are part of the reason we are attracted to each other in the first place. So instead of knocking heads together, we started to build on each other's strengths. In the process we discovered that each of these negative characteristics and hang-ups can be transformed into positive strengths.

For example, here's carefree old sanguine me coming home after a weekend family seminar. I can hardly wait to get home. And all the time I am driving I am thinking of all the neat things I want to do when I get home. No sooner do I get inside the door than I say, "Honey, let's do this, and this, and this." And lovely, organized, choleric Melba, with her strong will, responds with, "No, we're going to do that, and that, and that!" And immediately we are at an impasse.

But now we understand each other's basic temperament. One of Melba's real strengths is her organization. So why don't I build on her strength? Now when I get some ideas, I make suggestions and then listen to her evaluation. I am tempering my impulsiveness with her discipline. And Melba is tempering her stubbornness with some of my emotional response to situations. And it's so neat.

Now just because we have learned something about each other's temperaments, all of our differences have not been resolved overnight. No, it's not that easy. But we have a place to begin—a starting reference point. And today our marriage is better than ever!

Can you imagine some of the problems that occur with other combinations of temperament? Can you see the explosive situation if a calm, placid, unflappable phlegmatic married a volatile choleric? Or what if a happy, carefree sanguine chooses to marry a moody, sensitive melancholic? Rough! Ow, I hurt thinking about the struggles ahead.

But with an understanding of the basic temperaments, you can identify the typical response to a situation. And if that response is not what you want from your spouse but is consistent with his or her temperament, you know it's not a dig at you. You can anticipate typical responses and work on strengths, rather than hang-ups, to smooth out the relationship.

Before you try to figure out what temperament all your friends and family possess, let me remind you again that no one is all one temperament. Some of us are 60%/40%. Others may be almost half-and-half. And then there are some who are predominately one temperament with only a trace of any of the others. Each of us is unique.

When it comes to our children, the basic temperament characteristics are present early and may be easy to identify. Part of the reason why tension can develop between one child and one parent is the conflict of different temperaments. As we will see in the next chapter, part of the reason why children have parents is to smooth off the rough edges, strengthen the weaknesses and defuse the hang-ups.

To Think About:
1. Look back at the illustrations for each temperament. Go through the lists of positive characteristics and negative hang-ups and identify your predominate temperament.
2. Do the same thing for each member of your family, beginning with your spouse and continuing with your children.
3. Have the other members of your family do the

same temperament evaluation about themselves. Discuss together any differences of
opinions.

Chapter
4

WHICH WAY
DO THEY GO?

Which Way
Do They Go?

I always told my kids when they were growing up that we made a lot of mistakes. But then I would remind them, "Kids, don't be too hard in judging us, we've never been parents before." There should be a training program for parents. At least they could tell us what *not* to say or do with our kids.

One of the principles we often hear quoted from the Bible is that we are to train up a child in the way he should go. But I always wondered which way do they go? When I discovered the idea of the different temperaments, I thought, "Aha, that means I should train them according to their temperament." And some of these different temperament traits show up early.

We have a guy on our camp staff who has a

three-year-old son. Mean? Oh, can that little kid ever be cruel. He baptized a cat this past summer. The last thing that poor animal remembered was an old-fashioned dunking that didn't stop. That little boy has choleric written all over him.

You may see the temperament traits even earlier than that. If you pull one of those pacifiers out of the mouth of some little babies, watch out! They'll start yelling and screaming and throw a regular fit. But if you take that precious thing away from some other little ones they may just look up at you as if nothing happened.

All three of our kids are different, even though each of them is an extrovert. Sandra, my oldest, is a sanguine mouth like I am. She is the only girl I know that comes into a room mouth first. And guess who she married? A perfect phlegmatic. We call him the "old super-phleg," and he loves it.

When their little boy came along, my first grandson, he took after his dad. Matthew is quiet, calm and just never gets excited. He's completely different from any kids I raised. He came over to our house one time when he was about two years old, and that day I came home excited about spending some time with my little grandson. I asked, "Where's Matthew?" Melba said, "He's out in the back yard." And immediately I could imagine him picking all the new flowers I had just labored over the previous weekend. I ran out back and much to my surprise, found phlegmatic little Matthew, standing there peacefully with his hands folded, admiring all the pretty flowers.

A couple of years later, Matthew had a sister. Guess who she is like? Her sanguine mother! And to see those two kids together is just like seeing their mom and dad together in miniature.

As a phlegmatic, Matthew loves to tease his little sister. But even though she is younger, she is also tough and stubborn. She can really stand her ground. She even punches Matthew out every so often to remind him he's not really in control. She has sanguine written all over her.

The temperament characteristics relate to the verse in Proverbs quoted earlier. It can also be translated "Train up a child according to his way, or temperament." As a parent, you need to treat each child differently, based on his or her own temperament. You don't treat a choleric the same way you treat a melancholic. I've observed some friends of mine disciplining their children. One child is a phlegmatic and seldom needs any physical punishment. His parents point out his misbehavior and the consequences, and before they have finished, he is repentant. But they can spank his choleric brother repeatedly without seemingly making a dent in his stubborn will.*

* For a more detailed study on temperament in children, I suggest you read *How to Develop Your Child's Temperament*, by Beverly LaHaye, published by Harvest House Publishers.

Another important difference that parents need to be aware of is the basic emotion that gives each temperament its motivation. Phlegmatics and melancholics are both motivated by fear. When our kids were little, I enjoyed playing with them by putting them on my hand and lifting them high into the air. They loved it. But the first time I tried this with little phlegmatic Matthew, his face turned white with fear. I don't think he took a breath until he was back on solid ground again.

Sanguines and cholerics are not bothered by fear. Remember Patton? He'd have fought the whole world by himself if necessary. Neither of these temperaments even know the meaning of the word fear. The motivating emotion for the extrovert is anger. If you want to get a sanguine moving, get him angry. I sure know the truth of this. The only time I get motivated to diet is when I get angry with my stomach for getting in the way when I attempt to tie my shoes.

In order to properly train up our children, we must begin with an understanding of their temperament and the basic emotion that motivates their behavior. To bring about a balance in the introverted temperaments, we must deal with their fear. And to create a sense of equilibrium in the extroverted temperaments, anger must be brought under control. A steady, consistent awareness of these basic tendencies is the starting point for each parent.

Lurking behind these potentially destructive

emotions is an even more basic problem—selfishness. The root of all sin is found in selfishness. For example, why does a man commit adultery? Out of concern for the woman? No, he's basically driven by his selfishness. You can go down the list of sins, and you will find that each one had its beginning in uncontrolled selfishness.

The fear of the introvert and the anger of the extrovert are both grounded in selfishness. The introvert is afraid that his neat little world will be modified by an outsider. He is fearful of any intrusion or of being forced outside of himself. The extrovert's anger grows out of his selfish resentment over something not going his way. This anger is centered around a very selfish ego that looks out for itself.

Wise parents begin the task of training up their child at a level that even supercedes the individual differences of temperament and introversion or extroversion. They go beyond these levels to the primary battleground of selfishness. Now the self is not bad. It is the selfishness of the self that is the problem. You know the early symptoms: "Mine, give it to me!" "No, it's mine, don't you touch it!" Only the words change as we grow up; the pattern stays the same.

I am aware that this runs contrary to popular opinion. There are many who still argue that humans are basically good and that all we need to do is allow each other to express our goodness. I saw a sign recently that expressed this philosophy. It was put up by the local police department and said, "Lock your car. Don't help a good boy go bad." Do you see the implication? Good boys can go bad only if they start out good.

A variation of that theme is that children are neither good nor bad but are only a product of their environment and their heredity. And does that ever put the pressure on parents and on society. If a person commits a crime, it's society's fault. I remember one of our well-known news reporters commenting at the end of a long trial in which a person was convicted of murder. He was a political assassin. This newsman told the American people, "You really cannot blame_____. In reality, we are all to blame. Society has failed."

Now there is a sense in which that is true, but I just can't accept that man's logic. Unfortunately, he is not alone in that opinion. But if you have checked the Bible, you will not be misled by these ideas. Isaiah 53:6 NAS says that, "All of us like sheep have gone astray, each of us has turned to his own way." And Psalms 58:3 KJV says that children are born lying from their earliest words. These are pretty tough statements, aren't they? And there are a lot more like them. Who's correct, the Bible or our modern-day experts? Well, do you have to teach a child to tell a lie? No. In fact, we go to a lot of effort to teach children to be honest. Lies seem to come with the product.

We have a friend who loaned us his beach

house for a week during the summer. It's a beautiful pad on the sand and surf. We were excited about getting away alone. But as soon as we moved in, we were joined by our oldest daughter and her family for the day. And innocent little blond-haired, blue-eyed Matthew walked in, found a large white wall and his crayons, and started being creative. I walked into the room just as he was adding a masterful stroke of red, and I yelled, "Matthew, you stop that!"

And boy, he wheeled around still holding that red crayon, looked up at me with his blue eyes and innocent face and said, "Matthew didn't do it." Oh, it was a good thing I was his grandfather because I just broke up. I thought to myself, "How incredible! How could that kid become a professional liar at the age of three?" His environment didn't teach him. But I guess you could say he inherited the ability, because we're all born that way. The Bible says we are fallen, sinful creatures. There is something inside of us that leads us in the wrong direction. And you can depend on it coming with every newborn baby.

Now don't get gloomy and give up. You don't have to be a pessimist or a prophet of doom to believe this. I'm an optimist, and this information fills me with hope! I believe the Bible because it explains the way we are. And if I know what I'm dealing with, I'm filled with confidence!

You see, when I accept the fact that my kids

are basically selfish and this shows itself either through misbehavior motivated by fear or anger, I know what my job is as a parent. If I'm going to train up my child in the way he should go, then I must first deal with selfishness. Otherwise, that kid will head off in the wrong direction. And if I understand the basic temperament of my child, I know his weaknesses and the emotion that causes those weaknesses. And with that knowledge, I'm ready to be a trainer.

But how do I go about training my child? By using two fundamental tools—restrictiveness and discipline.

To Think About:
1. Describe things that each of your children do that express either the basic emotion of fear or of anger. How do they express their selfishness?
2. How do you feel about the basic nature of children? Do your ideas agree with the behavior you observe in others? In yourself?
3. State at least two positive things you will do this week to help your children deal with either selfishness, anger or fear.

Chapter
5

THE TOOL
OF
RESTRICTIVENESS

The Tool
Of Restrictiveness

What kind of parent are you? Or better yet, what type of parent do you want to be? In a recent survey, parents were divided into four different categories based on how they handled what the researchers felt were the two basic tools that are absolutely necessary for good parenthood. These two essentials are support and control. Parents give either high or low support to their children. They are either high or low in their ability to control the behavioral pattern of their child.

When you take these two factors and place them on a grid, you come up with four different types of parents. The type of parent you are depends on how you handle support and control.

Permissive	Authoritative	High Support
Negligent	Authoritarian	Low Support
Low Control	High Control	

You can see that the *negligent parent* is low in both control and support. This often means that the parent really doesn't care about his kids. He offers them no quality input, spends little time with them, and exerts no control over their behavior. You could almost call him the absentee parent—he might as well not even be there.

You probably know some of his kids—they're the ones who never have to be home for dinner, have no curfew at night and are ready to move in with you if you show them any love and concern.

Obviously, I have just described the more extreme example. This would be the parent who is in the bottom left hand corner of our grid.

Some negligent parents might show a little more support and concern, or exert a little more control than the parent in our example, but each of them would be characteristically negligent.

The parent who is high in support but low in control is called the *permissive parent*. This is the kind of parent who spends a lot of quality time with his children. The kids know they are loved and that their parents support them in what they do. But when it comes to placing any controls on the behavior of their children, these parents fall apart.

If the principal from school called this type of parent on the phone and said, "Your boy is in trouble, we need a conference," he would probably respond by saying, "Not *my* boy!" Permissive parents are very defensive, very protective and very supportive of their children. But they just can't seem to control their behavior.

When these parents visit your home with their kids, you can easily recognize them. You'll probably have mixed feelings about the visit. They're fun people to be with, but their kids drive you crazy because their parents never correct their behavior. In fact, you almost wonder if they even know what their kids are doing. Oh yes, sometimes in the middle of a conversation, the mother will look over at Betsy bouncing on your new sofa and say, "Betsy, honey, please don't do that." And then she'll pick up the conversation where she left off, apparently oblivious to the fact that Betsy never stopped. In fact, she didn't miss a bounce! And you sit there wondering why this mother doesn't follow through on discipline.

The third box describes the kind of parents who are called *authoritarian parents*. Since they use the General Patton approach, they are very high in control. Their kids are well behaved when a parent is around, but when Pop's away, watch out!

These parents act like dictators with their kids. You almost get the feeling the kids exist so that they can be bossed around by Mom and Dad. These parents are very high on behavioral control, but support is non-existent. These are the legalistic parents who have a rule for every situation but never have any time to visit the school on Open House night, or attend a Little League game, let alone help coach the team. Usually, their children are fairly well behaved when they are with them, but are not secure enough to be able to handle themselves when the boss is gone.

Now the style that came out on top is that of the *authoritative parents*. Here the parents came out high on both the ability to control their children's behavior and to give them support. These parents earn the right to be the leaders of their children by spending quality time with them and disciplining them fairly. So the children learn to respect their parents as leaders.

Kids can spot these kinds of parents. Other kids enjoy being in their home. There is no hesitancy about coming to these adults for advice. The kids will say, "Dad, what do you think about this?" and know that Dad will take the time to give an honest and thoughtful opinion.

Where do you fit on this grid? Where does your spouse fit? Remember, very few of us are really way out in the corners, but most of us are probably scattered around some place closer to the middle.

Now the problems develop when you have an authoritarian father and a permissive mother. And the principle of opposites attracting each other seems to work here as well as with temperaments and so does the "law of repulsion." The father tends to become more authoritarian to make up for the mother's permissiveness, or vice-versa. And the tougher the father gets on the kids, the more permissive the mother becomes in order to compensate for the father.

Melba and I had a form of that problem. For example, when it came to money, I was tough. The kids never came to me for extra money; they always went to Melba. She was the "soft touch." And kids sure can learn that in a hurry. That attitude carried over into other areas as well. If one of our boys fell down, and if I didn't see blood, I'd say, "Get up, be a man!" But Melba— "Oh, my poor baby, does it hurt?"

If this is carried too far, it can really become destructive. The whole area of authority comes under attack. Father prepares to leave for work and before going out the door he tells his son, "I want the lawn mowed before I get home tonight." After he leaves, the permissive mother steps into the picture and says, "Aw, honey, your dad didn't really mean that. Mommy will help you get it done." In the process, she is undermining the role of the father and teaching the child to ignore what the father says. The "law of repulsion" can be devastating when it operates in the area of authority.

So how can you get a set of parents, who may be functioning from different sectors on our parents' grid, to work together as a team? I believe the key is to be the kind of "trainers" who understand how to be restrictive in the child's early years. These are the important foundation years, when the biggest blocks are laid in the building of the mind, the heart and the personality of the child. And this is the time that parents must be restrictive and work together as a team.

Now how do I mean "restrictive?" The word may seem to convey a negative feeling, but I want to use it in the same sense as a basketball or football coach is restrictive. Why does the coach insist that the players eat certain kinds of food, be in bed by ten, have a certain kind of haircut, and workout with the team so many hours each day? Because the coach is a mean ogre? He may be, but his reasons are based on the desire to be a winner and to perform at a peak level. He is restrictive so that the team can win the bigger prize—the championship.

That's how I want to use the word restrictive. I restrict my kids in order to develop certain lines of discipline in their lives, so they can enjoy life, and we can enjoy it with them. As they grow, we become more and more permissive in giving them privileges, especially as they display an increasing sense of personal responsibility. Unfortunately, many parents turn this around. They are permissive in the early years, and then, when the kid hits adolescence, they tighten down the clamps. And that just doesn't work!

Parents who turn this restrictive-permissive pattern around during the child's early years fit either the permissive or negligent parent role. These are the parents who watch the kid kick out the slats in the side of his crib and say, "Oh, look at little Willie. Isn't he cute kicking the slats out of the side of his bed!" But when Willie grows up and goes next door on his twelfth birthday and starts kicking the slats out of the neighbor's house, it's no longer funny. Suddenly the parents come down on Willie with both feet and threaten him. But often the kid doesn't respond. The pattern's been reversed and that can prove fatal!

Once I was speaking in the Chicago area and was staying with a youth minister and his family. He was sharp. He had a beautiful wife, beautiful home, beautiful car, beautiful kids, and I thought, "Wow, this guy's really got it together. Only 26 years old and he's got everything going for him." When he took me to his home, he introduced me to his wife and two kids and said, "Mr. Poure, your room's over there and here's the bathroom. We'll be eating in thirty minutes." Beautiful! Just like clockwork. I was impressed.

I picked up my suitcase and took about two steps before I heard the wife say to the little guy, "Joey, wash your hands." The next thing I heard was a thump and the mother going "Ow-w-w-w-w-w-w!" When I turned around I realized that little Joey had just kicked his mother in the shin with his tough little leather shoe. She grabbed him and pulled him into the bathroom. I did a quick double take and headed to my room.

Thirty minutes later I reappeared and joined the family at the dinner table. Everybody was at the table except Joey. He was over watching TV and we were sitting and waiting. Now at my house, when we sit down to eat, we pray and then we eat—no fooling around. But this was a bit different. Finally the father said, "Joey? Will Joey come to the table to eat?" "Yes, Daddy," he answered as he pushed the off button and came running to the table.

But then we waited for at least another fifteen seconds after Joey sat down. Now, I can assure you that fifteen seconds is a very long time when you're hungry. This time the father said, "Joey, can Daddy pray?" The little guy answered,

"Yes, Daddy." So we prayed, and finally we ate. Everything went smoothly, and when we finished the meal the father again asked, "Joey, can Daddy have devotions?" Again, Joey gave the right answer and we moved ahead with the devotions.

I'd never been exposed to this kind of thing before and I was beginning to think all of this was rather strange. But I reminded myself that I was a guest in their home. After devotions were finished, I picked up my dishes (just as my wife has trained me to do) and carried them into the kitchen. As I did, I asked the wife, "Did you tell your husband that Joey kicked you in the leg?" "Oh, no," she answered as she looked down at the spot on her leg that was already turning black-and-blue. Well, I just forced my way into their business as I continued, "Why didn't you?" "You don't understand," she replied, "they have such a beautiful father-and-son relationship. I just don't want to do anything that would mar it!"

I was about ready to mar little Joey's behind, but I managed to control myself and stay quiet on the subject for two more days. All during that time when I was in the home, I observed the father asking Joey for permission to do everything. And I finally figured out the problem. Because the father said everything to his son in the form of a question, Joey got the idea that he was running his father—in fact, running the family—because he gave Dad the okay on everything! But when the mother talked to Joey, she didn't ask him, she told him to do something. And Joey didn't like that!

Finally I sat down with the father and told him about the kicking episode. "Not MY son!" he protested. "Listen," I assured him, "I've been living with you for several days and I'm telling you what I saw. I was there. And I'm not trying to stir up trouble or cause any waves, but...." and I told him what I thought the problem was. I was very bold with him because I felt certain that he and his wife could handle it. They had so many other things going for them.

But can you imagine what would happen the first day little Joey went to kindergarten? Picture the scene: Little Joey walks in and checks everything out. It's time for class to begin and the teacher says, "Joey, sit down . . . Ow-w-w-w-w-w!" And that would only be the beginning of problems. The parent who is low in control during the early years of the child's life often creates an impossible problem during adolescence because he just can't reverse the pattern. Restrictiveness is the watchword of the pre-teen years, and then comes a progressive permissiveness that prepares the child for adulthood. But that's the subject of the next chapter and we're not finished here yet.

Restrictive training begins from birth onward. Kids need to know where the lines are drawn and what the rules are. Sometimes we adults react against the idea of rules and laws, but without law, there can be no real freedom. No one is totally free in a society. If you lived alone on your own island, you could be totally free. But as soon as another person moved on to the island, you would have to negotiate your respective freedoms.

Alone, you can run around in your birthday suit, spit into the wind, throw things, and no one else is there to care. But with two people, you must decide where your freedom ends and the other person's freedom begins. If you have four people, you've got a more complicated problem. And when you have several million people, freedoms must be controlled by laws.

Now the interesting thing is that laws seem to formulate within the situation. For example, a little kid is crawling around exploring the house. He discovers a fascinating glass vase and starts to reach out and touch it. Mother says "No, don't touch that." The kid hears the voice and backs off for a moment. Then he reaches again. This time mother explodes, "I said, don't touch that!" The kid backs off again. Several moments later he reaches again. "I SAID, DON'T TOUCH THAT!!" The kid cringes a bit and backs away. But again his curiosity takes over, and he reaches out the fourth time. SMACK!! "I SAID NO!!!" And the kid retreats, rubbing his hand or the back of his head.

This child has just been trained. What did he learn? He learned a new law: three grunts and then duck. That's not restrictive training. That is the type of control characteristic of the authoritarian parent who is high in control and low in support. And the thing that usually accompanies this type of discipline is an unpredictable arbitrariness.

In our family, we had our laws, only we called them traditions. Sometimes our traditions were only one day old, but we still called them traditions. And we developed a three-phase method of implementing these traditions to provide some restrictive training. Here's how it worked.

The same kid is approaching the fascinating glass vase. Only this time the mother simply says, "No" as the little guy reaches for it. That's phase one. And if you are consistent in your use of this three-phase program, phase one is often sufficient. If it isn't, you move into phase two.

Phase two takes some loving effort on the part of the parents. You can't just sit there and yell. If Junior reaches for the vase again, you must get up, go over to where he is, look him in the eye and explain to him that he is not to touch the vase because it is very fragile and may get broken. And then you say, "Now if you touch that vase again, here's what will happen to you." And you explain phase three.

Let's use another illustration. Your little three-year-old has just run out into the street. That calls for phase two to be implemented immediately—assuming you have a tradition that says playing in the street is a no-no. You and your child have an intimate meeting as you explain why playing in the street is a no-no. As you finish your explanation, you remind your child about phase three: "Now if you go out into the street again, here is what I will do to you . . . And you expand on what comes next.

The child may not even understand the words as you explain why he is not to play in the street, but he will pick up the idea very quickly from the tone of your voice that this is something he is not supposed to do. Your own attitude will convey more than your words.

The problem with phase two, for many parents, is that it takes time and effort. You must get out of your comfortable chair and have a meeting of the minds with your kid. That's part of being a restrictive trainer—a good coach. And it is also necessary that you follow through on phase three, or else phase two will be meaningless.

Phase three involves punishment. It might be a restriction. My dad would make me go into the house and sit looking into a corner for thirty minutes. That's a long time for a little kid, but it was sure effective. "Go sit in that chair and look at the wall for thirty minutes," he'd say, adding, "and think about what you did!" Boy, I sure got the message.

In my home, phase three involved up to five swats on the behind, depending on the offense. If one of our kids got to phase two, we would explain the consequences: "Now if you do that one more time, you'll get three swats on the bare bottom." And the number of swats was determined by the size of the offense.

You're thinking, "Mr. Poure, that's primitive!" But do you know where I got the idea? That's right, from the owner's manual. I read, "Discipline your son in his early years while there is hope. If you don't you will ruin his life" (Proverbs 19:18 TLB) and, "Don't fail to correct your children; discipline won't hurt them! They won't die if you use a stick on them!" (Proverbs 23:14 TLB). And when I read, "He that spareth his rod hateth his son" (Proverbs 13.24 KJV), I decided to follow the directions. This is from the Bible!

I think what we are seeing today is a reaction against the cases of parental brutality. We watch a series on TV about how some parents batter their kids; so we react by saying, "I'm not even going to lay a finger on my kid." You see, that's our tendency. We move from one extreme to the other. Well, obviously I am not advocating that you be brutal with your children. The Bible always talks about physical punishment in the context of love:

> "My son, don't be angry when the Lord punishes you. Don't be discouraged when he has to show you where you are wrong. For when he punishes you, it proves that he loves you."
> Hebrews 12:5,6 TLB

Now that sounds incongruous to some parents. They say, "I love my children too much to spank them." The Bible says that love requires discipline and correction, and that sometimes must include a spanking. Notice the next verses in Hebrew 12:

"Let God train you, for he is doing what any loving father does for his children. Whoever heard of a son who was never corrected? If God doesn't punish you when you need it, as other fathers punish their sons, then it means that you aren't really God's son at all—that you don't really belong in his family."

Hebrews 12:7,8 TLB

The writer of these words then goes on to say that discipline and correction are never pleasant. So don't expect it to be. But it's needful.

Now to discipline in love means that when I am correcting my child physically, or psychologically, the highest intention in my conscious mind is to promote the welfare and the training of that child. Love means that I am more interested in the kid's welfare than I am in releasing my own frustrations. If I'm only releasing my frustrations, I am simply teaching my kid to duck quick because I'm bigger than he is.

My father, bless his heart, took a long time to

get mad, but when he did, oh baby, you'd better move! We've talked together about this; so what I am telling you is no family secret. Many times by dad would grab my brother and me after we'd come home from church. He'd pick us off the ground and shake us and say, "Why don't you boys act like Deacon's boys?" Well, we learned to get away quick. We didn't know how Deacon's boys were supposed to act. So we tried to find out. Then we learned to be actors. When my dad was around, we were nice little boys—"Yes, sir! No, sir!" We'd drive past a liquor store and we'd say, "Oh, look at that evil liquor—evil, evil, evil!" We knew that would please dad because he was always talking about the evils of alcohol. And dad would say, "Well done, sons, very wise boys."

You know how I learned to avoid that pattern with my kids? I discovered how *after* I had received a ticket from the California Highway Patrol one morning. I'll never forget it. My driving record wasn't the greatest, and if I got one more ticket within a twelve-month period my insurance rate would go up.

This particular Saturday morning I was driving up the freeway toward Pasadena going to a Family Seminar. It was early in the morning and I had plenty of time. But my mind was already at the seminar, thinking of what I was going to say. And the next thing I knew, two big strawberries appeared in my rear view mirror going "poingo, poingo, poingo." My heart sank, for this was the eleventh month into my year. I was really ticked at ME as I pulled over.

This big moosey, gigantic patrolman—probably six foot six—came up along side my car. He stood there with his hat and waited while I rolled down my window. "Good morning," he said, "Got any idea how fast you were going?" I told him I didn't really because I was thinking about something else. Well, he took my license and wrote out the ticket while I sat there burning inside because of my carelessness.

Finally the patrolman finished his writing, shoved the papers through the window and said, "Mr. Poure, would you please sign here? All this means is that you must appear in court within ten days." I took the ticket silently, scrawled my signature and handed it back to him. He ripped out my copy and stuck it back through the window. I reached up to take the ticket away from him, but he didn't let go. All the time I tugged at the ticket I didn't look at this guy. I just sat there staring at my shoes.

Finally, I got the idea that he wanted me to look at him. So I looked up this big long arm. The moment my eyes caught his, he let go, backed off, put his hat back on and said, "Mr. Poure, remember, speed kills. We want you around on our freeways for a long time. Slow down and live, and have a good day." And he went back to his car.

As I drove away, I told God, "Dear Lord, help me to learn something from this—something more than just how to rejoice in tribulation.

Teach me, Lord." And as I was driving I was saying to myself, "Why, as a dad, can't I be like that cop? Why can't I be cool when my kids are in trouble instead of blowing my stack?" Then I started asking myself why that cop was so cool. And I figured they trained him to be that way in Cop School. He premeditated exactly what he was going to do!

Can you imagine what would have happened if that cop had acted like many parents do when their kids do something wrong? What if he had walked up to my car yelling, "YOU STUPID IDIOT, WHAT DO YOU THINK YOU'RE DOING? . . ." Why I'd have jumped out of my car and gone for him, and one of us would have been dead. But he was so calm and in control of his behavior.

Driving along I prayed, "Lord, help me to discipline my kids that same way." When I got home, Melba and I developed this idea. Whenever we came to phase three, we would say to our child, "Go to your room." We did this for our sake. It gave us time to cool down, get calm, have a little time to talk to the Lord, and then, when we had our emotions under control, we would go to visit him in his room.

We had a lot of practice in this with our son Mark. He'd go to his room and sit. Finally, I would walk in and just sit down without saying a word. I'd look at him—sympathetically. Did you ever notice how, when your kid is in trouble, he just won't look at you. Mark was that way. Then I would say, "Mark, why do you want a spanking?" And every time he'd come off the side of his bed and say, "Dad, I don't want a spanking, honest!" Then I would remind him of what led up to our moving to phase three. For instance, if he had been late, I'd say something like, "Mark, you told me you wanted a whipping. Remember what happened yesterday when you were late getting home? You had to sit in the corner for thirty minutes. (Or whatever the restriction was.) And do you remember that I told you if you came home late one more time that you were in phase three?" And he'd say, "Yeah." "Well, Mark, when you came home late again, you were telling me you wanted spanked."

That's hard for kids to get a hold of, I know. But what you are doing here as a parent is putting the burden of their behavior on their own shoulders. And that's exactly what you have to do. You begin to build personal integrity, based upon personal responsibility, into their lives. And that must start early!

Mark and I would talk about the situation until I felt he understood that the spanking was a direct result of his behavior. Then I'd ask, "Mark, what's that worth? How many?" And he'd always answer, "That's a one-er." Now if it was a first time offense in phase three, it might be a one-er or a two-er. If it was a third offense, then three swats, and so on, up to five. But hopefully you never need to go that far. They seem to get the message before that's necessary.

We found an effective way to handle our other boy. David was tough and had high pain tolerance. If my wife gave him a spanking, he'd turn around and say, "Ha, ha. Didn't hurt!" It drove her out of her mind. Finally, we had to figure out how we could better handle phase three with him—not just to make it hurt, but in order to make the point.

What we learned, we started doing with each of the kids. And it may sound a bit corny to you, but it worked. Believe me, it made the difference. When it came time to administer the spanking, we were never in a hurry. Before we applied the rod to the seat of learning, we'd pray with them. Nothing long, just a brief prayer that they would understand that the spanking was meant to help them and that, through obedience, other spankings wouldn't be necessary. And then we'd use a little paddle we bought at the dime store. We never used a rod because that made welts. And we never used our hand, because we wanted our hands to be the hands of blessing with our kids.

After the spanking was finished, we'd always say, "Honey, when the sting goes away, you come and see me." And then we got out of the room and shut their door. In a few minutes they'd come to see us. And as soon as they got close, we'd look them in the eye and say, "Do you want to do that again?" That was the only time we asked that question. Then we'd take them in our arms and let them know we loved them.

Now that is biblical correction. If it sounds complicated to you, work at it. Once you get into disciplining your child this way, it becomes easier. And it's just so neat when it's done correctly. The exciting thing is that your kids will love you for it. Why? Because you're communicating to them that correction is being done for the right reason!

But there comes a time when all of this must change. The tools of the restrictive training are for the child. As the child grows into an adolescent, the traditions change. And this is the time for permissiveness—progressive permissiveness.

To Think About:
1. What type of parents are you? Place yourself somewhere on the grid at the beginning of the chapter. Discuss with your spouse where you think you both are on the grid and why.
2. What positive things are you doing with your children that could be called restrictive? Can they be both positive and restrictive?
3. Do you follow a plan when you discipline your children? Discuss with your spouse your system to better communicate to your children that discipline is meant to help them, not to relieve your frustrations?

Chapter
6

PROGRESSIVE
PERMISSIVENESS

Progressive
Permissiveness

Do you want your kids to grow up? I sure did!
I didn't want them sitting around my house the
rest of their lives. And we let them know it. Now
we didn't shove them out—don't get me wrong.
We just dropped subtle little hints now and then.
Like when Sandra was in the twelfth grade,
we'd ask her quite regularly what she was going
to do when she graduated. Once she said,
"Sometimes I get the feeling you want me to
move out." And we smiled back at her and
replied, "You're right."

We started our program when our kids first
became teenagers. Kids look forward to that
day. So we made it special. We had what we
called a "growing-up" party or a spiritual "bar
mitzvah." And from that point on we recognized

them as young men or young women.

Our oldest wanted us to allow her to go out on dates, even before she was a teenager. I assured her that was impossible, at least before she became a teenager. Then I realized that was only six months in the future. So I said, "Sandra, let me be your first date." She got very excited, but then she stopped and asked, "Really? You mean you'd take me out?" I informed her that not only would I take her out, but that we would go "top drawer."

So we had six months to get ready and we made a big to-do about it all. When her birthday arrived, her Mom took her down to the hairdresser and had Sandra's hair all done up fancy. Then she helped her with some make-up and some fancy toilet water. Of course, a new dress and some pantyhose and little high heels finished the job. She was beautiful. I borrowed a friend's Cadillac and bought Sandra a corsage and off we went.

What an evening! We went to a nice restaurant and had our picture taken by a waterfall. Every so often we pull out the picture and all of us just crack up. Great memories!

Anyway, while we were finishing our dinner, I said, "Sandra, I know you want to grow up, and your mom and I want to do everything we can to help you." Then I pulled out my pen and drew a box on the paper napkin. "Honey," I continued, "now you're a teenager, and we want to give you some new freedoms. I'm going to put some things inside this box and they will become your responsibility. You know how to take care of your room. But from now on this will be your responsibility. We believe you can handle it; so we're not going to say another word about your room to you. If you want to live in a pigpen, you can live in a pigpen." And her eyes got big as she realized I meant it.

DAVID'S RESPONSIBILITY:

G—To get a grade point average of 3.0 and a 90% in driver's education class.
Be home by 11:30.

(16 years old)
Poure Box or Birthday Box

Then I added, "Now here's what we're going to do with the box. When you turn fourteen, we want to give you a bigger box with more responsibilities and with more freedoms as well. And when you're fifteen, a bigger box, and so on until, when you're eighteen, there will be no box. You'll be free. Do you understand? And my beautiful little thirteen-year-old daughter said, "Yes, Daddy."

That's how we started using what we call the "Poure boxes," or the "birthday boxes," with our kids. There is a difference between the kind of permissiveness these boxes imply and the permissiveness that precedes the teen years. With progressive permissiveness, everything you put into the box as your child's responsibility is his *total responsibility*. So you need to be

careful what you put into the box. You see, prior
to the boxes, if I told one of my kids to take out
the trash and he didn't take it out, then I took it
out. But when the kids hit the teen years, there
was a new dimension of responsibility added—
total responsibility in progressively larger areas
of life.

The hook is that whatever goes into the
fourteen-year-old box is completely dependent
upon how well the child took care of his
thirteen-year-old responsibility. And you have a
whole year to work things out and discuss what
goes into the next year's box.

So what do you put inside the box? Well,
that's between you and your teen. Mark, my
youngest, was very well organized. Giving him
the responsibility for his bedroom would be no
challenge at all. So on his thirteenth birthday we
put a big M in his box. That stood for money. Up
to that point we had given him a little allowance
each week and his lunch money every day. But
when he turned thirteen, that all stopped.
Instead, we gave him five one-dollar bills every
Monday. Note—not Saturday, but Monday;
otherwise he'd never make it past the weekend.
Mark's task was to regulate his own budget. He
did it beautifully.

And along with the responsibility, you also put
some freedoms into the box. David, our middle
guy, wanted to drive the car when he turned
sixteen. So when he turned fifteen, I drew his
box and put a big G in it for grades. I said,

"David, I want you to get your grade point average up to 3.0, and I want you to get at least a 90% in your driver's education class. That's going to be your responsibility this year."

Do you know what he did? He got a 3.6 grade point average—higher than ever before or since. But because it was his responsibility, he made it. Kids respond to these long-range challenges if they know that their freedoms and privileges are related to them. And all the time, you are building responsibility into their lives.

If children aren't allowed to act responsibly, their character development is going to be stunted. It's just like tying your arm to your side for six weeks so you can't use it or move it. You'd have to work on strengthening it again. It is the same with responsible behavior. Your kids need to work on strengthening that characteristic early. Responsibility cannot be strengthened unless it is used. And that's the purpose of progressive permissiveness.

Another item we put into the box was the time the kids had to be home. This illustrates beautifully one of the advantages of progressive permissiveness. When my children were thirteen, they had to be in at 10:00 in the evening. (Of course, exceptions were made for special occasions.) Each year we added 30 minutes extra to the time they could spend on their night out. By the time they got to be seventeen, the magic hour was midnight. And of course, at eighteen, there were no boxes or time limits.

Say you have two teenagers and your

thirteen-year-old says, "Why can Bobby stay out till 11:30 when I have to be in at 10:00?" "Easy," you answer, "When you get to be Bobby's age, you can stay out until 11:30—you'll have that freedom." Of course, you can set your own times and traditions (rules) to fit your own family. But the boxes work!

There was another tradition we had in our family concerning the curfew. If the kids were supposed to be home by 11:30 and they didn't make it until 12:00, we'd knock 30 minutes off their next outing. Unless, of course, they had problems and phoned.

When Sandra was dating the guy she eventually married, they played the time-game to the letter. When she was seventeen, they arrived home at the stroke of midnight. We started calling her Cinderella because she was so exact. It was wild. Then on her eighteenth birthday, I took her out and talked with her and gave her total freedom—she could come home any time she wanted. Guess what they did? They were home at 10:30 or 11:00 every time! How hard they must have tried to stay out until midnight before. And after they had their freedom, they proved the value of progressive permissiveness. Their freedom didn't go to their heads.

What if your child flunks his box? Well, then you simply erase the next year's box and redraw the previous year's box. If it were my kid, I'd say something like, "Well, you know it's really not our fault. It's yours. You didn't take care of this simple responsibility like we KNEW you could; so we can't give you any more freedom." Here again, the burden of responsibility is on his shoulders.

But I think you'll find that kids rise to the challenge. In fact, with Sandra, we didn't know what to put into her box when she turned sixteen. She was doing such a good job. So we suggested, "Sandra, why don't you put some things down on a piece of paper that you would like as freedoms, and we'll try to think of some corresponding responsibilities for your birthday."

Well, the next day we got a little note that said, "The only thing I would like to have is the freedom to choose where I go on my dates, even church." And that was all. Melba and I looked at each other and sort of gulped because we didn't really know what she meant by all that. I said, "Well, she's done a good job each year . . ." So we asked the Lord to give us some guidance that night. The next morning we still felt Sandra could handle it; so on her birthday we said, "You're on."

Oh, that was a shakey feeling. She was only sixteen and it was her choice to go anywhere she wanted to go. She still had her time limit and we had to check out who she went out with, but she could go anywhere.

We were two weeks into the deal when she got a telephone call from one of her girlfriends. Her friend wanted her to go to a Friday Nighter, a school-sponsored dance, down in what is now called Narc Park. It's "doper's heaven" in our town. Sandra leaned around the corner and said, "Daddy, my friend wants me to go to the Friday Nighter. May I?" I was sitting there reading my paper, and from behind the pages I said, "Honey, you just ask the Lord what you should do. Remember on your birthday we told you that you have the freedom to go where you want to go. So you just ask the Lord and whatever He says to you is fine with us." And before I could congratulate myself on the fine job I had done in handling that one, Sandra let out a squeal and said into the phone, "I'll go, I'll go, I'll go." She didn't even take time to ask the Lord.

Oh, I wanted to pull rank on her so bad I could taste it. I had to bite my tongue to keep quiet. She came by and leaned over my paper to give me a kiss—I was still staring at the paper, not seeing a single word—and then she said, "Good-bye, Daddy." You can believe that she knew what was going on inside her dad! She knew me like the back of her hand. And she knew I was steaming inside. But I just sat there silent.

"Would you pick us up at eleven?" she asked sweetly as she got to the door. "Yeah, I'll pick you up," I answered glumly. And off she went while I sat there with my paper covering up my agony.

About this time I heard some footsteps coming

into the room. Ah, here was Melba—my wife and helpmate, my tower of strength. But not a sound came from her mouth. I was still sitting there looking at my paper and I could see through that little opening at the bottom. I saw my wife's two feet, and she was shifting her weight back and forth on them. Nonverbal language—I knew I had problems. So I slowly, very slowly, let the paper come down until our eyeballs met across the top of the page. She was standing there with her hands on her hips, waiting. And as soon as our eyeballs met, she said, "Big box, BIG DEAL!"

Oh, I tell you, leadership is lonely. I don't remember what I said or did, but I do remember that Sandra called in less than an hour and I almost shouted with joy when I heard her ask, "Daddy, would you come and get me? This placed is weird." My heart was soaring as I told Melba. She let out a little squeal of delight as I ran to the car and took off to get our daughter.

All the way to the park, I thought to myself, "Now which sermon should I use on her?" And as I turned the last corner, I had one all picked out. But then the Spirit of God told me something. How do I know when God's talking to me? Very simple. When God tells me something, it's always diametrically opposite of what I have just decided. And this time He said, "Poure, keep your mouth shut!" I'd never say that to myself!

So when Sandra jumped into the car, I simply said, "Hi." And we drove on towards home.

Finally, she couldn't take it any longer. Her mouth is even more gregarious than mine. And when I didn't give her a sermon, she asked, "Well, Daddy, don't you want to know what happened?" I responded calmly, "Sure, Honey, if you want to talk about it." And all the way home I listened as she related what she saw, the influence it had on her and her reaction to it all. But what I really heard were some personal convictions. Melba and I both learned that night that God can lead our kids to conclusions, convictions, and standards, just as He does us, if we'll give Him a chance.

I know it's kind of scary, but I believe the only way for parents to survive the adolescent years is to have this kind of confidence. Sure we have had our defeats. We've wept in the night wishing we could undo some of our kids' mistakes. I will do everything I can as a parent to help my kids, but their behavior is their own responsibility.

Some parents play the blame-game if their kids have problems. We all make mistakes and many times we could do better. But I believe God is at work in every situation. Sometimes all you can do is pray that your kids make it. Peer pressures can be so great that kids will mess themselves up in spite of everything their parents do. But if the pattern is correct—if you begin with restrictiveness and move to progressive permissiveness—you're giving your kids the best chance they can have.

You say your son or daughter is already fifteen, and you wonder if it's too late to begin with the boxes? I don't think it is. Just sit down and explain to your kids that you're interested in seeing them grow up. Tell them that you have discovered something that has helped some other kids and you're going to use it in your family. Then draw the boxes and work out a fair exchange of responsibilities for freedoms. Be consistent as you work it out together. Now let's consider what it means to build character during these permissive years.

To Think About:
1. Think over how you usually treat your teen.
2. How often do you still treat him or her like a child?
2. How could you use the "Poure boxes" with your kids? What responsibilities and what freedoms would you put into a box for each of your teens?
3. Where do you have the greatest trouble being permissive with your kids? Why is it so hard to trust them in that area?

Chapter
7

RIGHT'S RIGHT
AND
WRONG'S WRONG

Right's Right
and
Wrong's Wrong

One of the exciting things I discovered about progressive permissiveness is the way it helps develop character in your teen. And an important aspect of the development of character is the ability to discern right behavior from wrong behavior.

For example, is it right or wrong to go to church? Is it right or wrong to smoke? How about smoking pot? Is it alright to gamble? Does the Bible actually say, "Thou shalt not gamble?" How about hair length? How long is right and how long is wrong? Or can that even be decided? If you've ever struggled with any of these or other issues, you know how confusing it can get. It's not like the good old days when the good guys all wore white hats and the bad guys always wore black. Things were a bit easier to decide back then, at least when it came to dividing up the cowboys.

I was speaking at a weekend camp last fall, and I heard that one of the kids at the camp was busted for possession of heroin. Well, there were only about a hundred guys there, so I started looking through the crowd to see if I could figure out who he was. I kept looking for some weird kid, but when I was introduced to him I was surprised to meet Mr. Straightsville! He looked like he was fresh out of the front row in Sunday School. You just can't tell anything by looks anymore.

So you ask, "What makes the right thing right and the wrong thing wrong?" Parents need to know the answer to this question so they can be better equipped to train their kids in this area.

Now there are some things that are always right and are never wrong. It is always right to love God. It is always right to love and honor our parents. And some things are always wrong, like stealing. Sometimes a person has a good reason for stealing—if his children are starving and he can't get any money. But it is still morally wrong to steal.

But usually our problems with right and wrong are not in this area. We run into difficulties in the relative space between the absolutes of right and wrong—the gray area. Several years back there was a song called "Shades of Gray." The basic message of that song is that there are no black and whites anymore; everything is a shade of gray. Some of these gray areas present valid questions because they relate to situations where two absolutes are in conflict. How do you help your kids make mature moral decisions in these areas?

Well, I've solved this for myself by placing everybody in the world on one of four levels. And everyone who makes a decision in the area of right and wrong makes it on the basis of certain propositions that are characteristic of his level of living. Let's look at these four levels.

The first level—the lowest level of behavior— is called the *natural level*. These are the people who decide everything according to their natural impulses, natural drives and natural instincts. This is the philosophy of hedonism. If it feels good, do it! A professor at a leading university wrote a book based on this level of behavior and titled it, *Let Your Glands be Your Guide*. That's too much!

Obviously, there are some decisions which can be made at this level and be considered good decisions. But we are talking about moral decisions. The people who make moral decisions on this natural level end up believing that the greatest good in life is personal pleasure. And that offers an empty future.

The next level is what I call the *social level*. On this level, decisions are made according to what society thinks and feels. What is everybody else doing? What will other people think? These are the important considerations of people operating at this level. Social pressures determine what they will wear today, how their hair will be styled, what color of junk they'll smear around their eyes and even the shape of the glasses they wear. The "in" group determines what everyone will do.

This approach appeals to our sense of democracy. Right and wrong can be decided by majority rule. But that's not democracy. This approach leads to all kinds of social pressures. Advertising appeals to this level—"*Everybody's* switching to Winston." Really? Can you see how corny that is when you stop to think about it? If *everybody* switched to Winston, they couldn't make enough Winstons to supply the demand. What does that kind of advertising do? Well, for one thing, it attempts to make you feel a little weird if you don't smoke Winston. That's social pressure!

Our kids are facing this pressure. This peer pressure is probably the greatest single pressure they face. And the tragedy is that peer pressures can often undo everything the parent has done up to that point. Some kids get into trouble and their parents embark on a great guilt trip. "Oh, we failed," they say, but they have a difficult time finding where they really did go wrong. I think kids today get into trouble more as a result of this social peer pressure than as a result of parental failure.

It's hard for adults to understand the

pressure involved when a group of kids say, "Hey, come on, chicken . . ." or "Why not, weirdo? What's the matter, scared?" To a developing, insecure adolescent, that can be devastating! As parents, we need to understand the reality of that pressure and do everything we can to help prepare our kids to go beyond making decisions at the social level and to move on to the next level.

The third level of behavior is the *moral level*. People living on this level make decisions, not by natural instinct or social pressure, but by conscience. There are a lot of wonderful people, both Christians and non-Christians, who operate on this level. And they make moral decisions that shame some of us. They march for cancer, work for the Red Cross, donate time to community projects, and do all kinds of other beautiful things.

The people who are living on this level make moral decisions based on the effect their decision will have on someone else. People at the first two levels make moral decisions based on selfish interests—like how it will feel or how they will look in the eyes of their peers. But at this third level, decisions are based on the influence they will have on the good of other people.

For example, if a moral person is a smoker and he is in a room with other people, he will ask, "Do you mind if I smoke?" He is sensitive to how his behavior might affect someone else.

My wife had an interesting encounter with someone who did *not* characterize this attitude. We were going out to eat with some friends and when we arrived at the restaurant, we had to wait a few minutes for a table. As we sat around the fire-circle waiting, all of a sudden a great puff of cigar smoke engulfed us as we talked. And I mean, it engulfed us.

About the time the second cloud covered us, I got a jab in my side and my wife said to me out of the side of her mouth, "Will you tell that guy to put out his cigar RIGHT NOW?" And she was ticked. I tried to assure her we would be waiting only a few minutes longer and said, "Be cool, Melba. You won't die, just be cool for another minute or so."

I turned back to talk with our friends, and suddenly I heard my wife's voice. She spoke in an uptight tone, "Do you want to chew my gum?" My brain went into a spasm and I spun around to see what was going on. And there was my wife, with her gum out of her mouth, talking to this suave-looking guy with the cigar. He had this stunned look on his face as she repeated her question, "Do you want to chew my gum?" Finally he got his answer out, "No thank you, Ma'am, not really." And she said to him, "Well, I don't want to smoke your cigar either. Will you please put it out!"

Obviously, this guy wasn't operating at the third level, but then I'm not too sure where Melba was coming from on that one either. But it worked!

The fourth and highest level is what I call the *Christian level.* I say this is the highest level because Christians are related to God. How good is God? He's perfect! And that puts the pressure on us as His children. And the world looks at the Christian and says, "All right, that's nice that you say you're a Christian, whatever that means. We really don't care what you say, we want to check out what that means in terms of your behavior." Making moral decisions on the Christian level involves behavior! And that raises a question that has bugged us for centuries: What does a Christian do that's different from everyone else?

In trying to resolve this question, some people have set up a behavioral code that describes the life-style of the Christian—what to wear, what to say or not say, where not to go, etc. Others reject any attempt to establish standards. While the discussion continues, it is important to recognize that many of the things included in this code are valid, because life-style, which even includes what you wear, does say a lot about a person.

For example, let's say that you are a salesman working in the very competitive market of downtown Los Angeles. And you walk into one of the big corporations dressed in a suit with narrow lapels, a pencil-thin tie with a tie clip, baggy pants, and a worn out briefcase that is obviously from a different era. You walk up to the receptionist and announce, "My name is _____ and I am here to speak to your purchasing director about some of the latest equipment available on the market today." Chances are you won't even get past the secretary! And you'll make good conversation at coffee break.

Now I am not saying that is right or proper. But it is a fact of business life. If you want to sell the latest equipment, you'd better look up-to-date yourself. What you look like, the way you fix your hair, the style of clothes you wear, the places you choose to attend—all of these say something about you to other people. You need to be aware of this.

But making decisions and living life at the Christian level goes beyond these things to a basic responsibility that is based on a very personal relationship between you and God. And the Bible—the owner's manual—becomes your guidebook. Let's see how this works:

Suppose someone asked me if it would be right or wrong to have an after-dinner cocktail. Here's how I would answer. If you're on the natural level, you go by instinct. So if it feels good, drink it. If you're on the social level, you ask if society approves. Do they? Sure, the majority does, anyway.

What about the moral level? Do moral people drink after-dinner cocktails? Sure. Some of them might not for various reasons, but many moral people do. What about the Christian level? Does the Bible say, "Thou shalt not drink after-dinner cocktails"? Not that I know of. Even the verse that says our bodies are the temple of the Holy Spirit does not preclude drinking a little alcohol anymore than it says we can't drink coffee or eat sweet desserts.

So you ask, "You mean to say, Ken, that you could even smoke marijuana and still be a Christian?" And to be honest with you, I would have to say, "At least in theory you could, because your relationship to Jesus Christ does not depend on what you do or what you don't do. If that were the case, then you could be saved by your own efforts." But don't go away, because I said "in theory." I believe my being a Christian *will* have an effect on what I do, for these reasons.

First of all, what controls my behavior on the Christian level? Jesus told His disciples, "But you shall receive power when the Holy Spirit has come upon you; and you shall be My witnesses . . ." (Acts 1:8 NAS). That means we are witnesses for Christ, wherever we are. So the question comes back to: Does this particular activity help me to be a positive witness for Christ to a non-Christian world?

I know a fellow who never really understood this. He attended one of the great Bible colleges in our country and even graduated. But this is one point he never got a hold of. His name was Earl. About five years after graduation, he had finally departed from his conservative brethren, split from his wife, and started living in a "pad" with two or three different gals. He called me up one time and asked me to visit him at his beach house.

I arrived at his "pad" and knocked at the door. Earl opened the door and stood there, looking funny as ever with strange little glasses and equally strange looking clothes. He invited me in and tossed me a pillow to sit on, for that was the major style of furniture in the place. "Earl," I said, "how's it going? I haven't seen you in four or five years." And he answered, "Baby, I'm God's favorite boy! I'm just praisin' the Lord every day." And I started to get this funny feeling that things weren't quite right.

We talked awhile and then he said, "Hey, let's drink to the glory of God," and he pulled out this wine jug and a couple of goblets. I told him, "Earl, you go ahead and drink it, but I can't drink it to the glory of God." And he started preaching at me, "That's what's wrong with you, Poure, you're hung up on legalism. That's what's wrong. You're hung up. You need to be free—like me!" His sermon was short, and my response was, "Earl, I'm free. I get drunk every time I want to. I just don't want to. There are two reasons why I won't drink with you. First, it's not a good witness to you, for you've already had too much. I can see that in your eyes. And second, I don't drink wine because I don't like it. To me it tastes like turtle-spit. And I'm free. My freedom is in the Spirit of God. It's just that He's changed my desires. That's *real* freedom!"

So there are a lot of things that I am free to do, even as a Christian, but because of my testimony I choose *not* to do them. And that's living beyond the rules. That's moving to the level of convictions.

Another principle from the owner's manual that helps decide issues for the Christian is found in I Corinthians 6:19 and 20: "Do you not know that your body is a temple of the Holy Spirit who lives within you, Whom you have received from God? You are not your own, you were bought for a price . . . So bring glory to Him in your body." (Amplified N.T.) That verse goes right along with what Paul said in Colossians 3:17 NAS: "And whatever you do in word or deed, do all in the name of the Lord Jesus, giving thanks through Him to God the Father." Whatever you're doing, it should glorify God, and you should be able to give thanks to God while you are doing it. That last part means you can pray a prayer of thanksgiving while doing what you are doing.

Anything you can't do with the spirit of thanksgiving is clearly wrong. For example, how could you pray, "Lord, I want to thank you; I want to pray this little prayer of thanksgiving, for the opportunity of cheating my government on my income tax"? I think you would choke on that kind of prayer, for it's rather obvious that cheating on your income tax is not a moral or Christian thing to do. That one is obvious. Now what about this example: "Lord, before we get into our petting session, we want to thank you for the ability to rub our bods together."

Your kids can see the point of that one, because you just can't pray that way. And if you can't honestly praise the Lord and thank God for what you are about to do, then you shouldn't be doing it. It's just that simple!

Before you hit your kids with that one, you might start easy. Take football. Is it right or wrong to play football? What does the natural level say? Sure. I spoke to the Los Angeles Rams before one of their games last season, and one of their linemen invited Christ into his life. He's got to be the biggest guy I've ever seen. I couldn't even put my two hands around his biceps. He told me he was part of what they call the "suicide squad." These are the four guys the team uses on run-backs. And all they do is "kill" the other guys. So on the natural level, football is great!

Is football right or wrong on the social level? Well, all you have to do is check out the attendance figures to find the answer to that one. Society loves football—if they play by the rules. Society wants the guys to wear helmets and the shirts that tell who they are. They also want the other guys down there with the funny striped shirts to keep things fair. That's all part of the social order that goes with a game like football.

How about the moral level? Do moral guys play football? Sure, but not all football players are moral. Some of the guys never get past the natural level. They are the ones who take cheap shots at the other guy or jam their cleats in the other guy's mouth when he's down. But the moral guy plays a clean game even if the referee isn't around. He's the type who knocks the runner down cleanly, then helps him get up and cleans the dust off his uniform.

How about the Christian level? Now watch this. I use football as an example because it is so neutral. Can an athlete be a positive witness for Christ? No doubt about it. Many of them are. What if an athlete's lips weren't controlled by the Spirit of God and every time he got into a tight situation, he took the name of God in vain. Could he become a negative witness? Sure. No doubt about it. So it could either be right or wrong for him to play football, depending on HOW he played. You can't make an out-and-out statement that it is always right, for he might be playing as a Christian for all the wrong reasons. It could be a real ego trip. Or he could be playing for the glory of God. And it would show by the way he kept the training rules and conducted himself on and off the playing field. And he could pray a prayer of thanksgiving before any game, that he would bring glory to God through his behavior.

My point is this: On the Christian level, you can't say flatly that something is right or wrong. You have to go below the surface and consider motives. That's why I say that you have to begin with some rules, but then you must move on to principles that will lead to convictions.

You can take any kind of behavior and run it through this test on the Christian level. Ask yourself three questions: (1) Will this behavior enhance my testimony for Christ? (2) Will this behavior bring glory to God? (3) Can I pray a prayer of thanksgiving for the opportunity to participate in this behavior? If you can answer "yes" to *all* three questions, then you can act confidently on the Christian level of behavior. If you have doubts at any point, I've found a simple formula that always works: When in doubt, DON'T!

One last word before we look at how we prepare our kids for marriage. It's obvious that we cannot communicate the Christian level of behavior to our kids if we are not attempting to live our own lives on that level. The old adage, "What you do speaks so loudly I can't hear what you say," certainly applies here.

To Think About:
1. Describe in your own words each of the four levels of moral behavior and decision making. Give an example for each level.
2. What moral decisions did you make this past week? At which level did you make each decision?
3. You could discuss these four levels of moral decisions with your child. Then create an opportunity for discussion together.

Chapter
8

PREPARING
YOUR KIDS
TO MARRY
IN HONOR

Preparing Your Kids To Marry In Honor

One of the biggest decisions our kids will make is the choice of a spouse. Next to their commitment to God, the greatest decision in the scope of influence on their future health, happiness and life is who they will choose to marry. And if we're going to give our kids the best chance at life, we need to help them in this area.

A good place to begin is with the definition of love. What is your definition? Is love a feeling? Can you be in love and not have a feeling? I've been married over thirty years and there is no one on earth that I love more than my wife, Melba. But right at this moment I have no "feelings"—no biological response—for her. Wait—let me check . . . No, I don't have one goose pimple anywhere on my body that says I am in love with her. Does that mean I'm not in love? Some people might think so, but I don't. Love is more than a feeling.

Kids are confused on this issue, and that confusion lies at the root of a lot of the problems in marriages today. The couple have such a great "feeling" for each other when they are going together, but when they get married, the feeling fades away. This is what we refer to when we say, "The honeymoon is over." Every couple goes through this experience when the feelings of infatuation must be transformed into maturing love because of the realities of living together. Unfortunately, when this transition isn't made, divorce is considered the only option. After all, what else is there to do when the "feeling" goes away?

I had a girl come up to me at camp one time after only two days on the grounds. She said, "Oh, Mr. Poure, I'm in *love*!" My quick question to her was, "How do you know?" "Oh," she answered, "whenever I see him, my heart begins to skip beats, and my hands begin to perspire, and I get hot flashes up the back of my neck." "Interesting," I told her, "and because of that you think you're in love?" "Yes," she said. I looked at her and said as gently as I could under the circumstances, "Honey, if you ran from this chapel over to the chow hall and back, you'd have exactly the same feelings. I don't think that's love." "I hate you," she said as she walked away.

Later on that week, I was talking to the kids about feelings and love, and I illustrated my point like this: Suppose I take an all-American boy and stand him in the middle of the room. And I have a lovely young girl come over and stand close to him. She runs her hands up the back of his neck, then runs her fingers through his hair as she blows into his ear and then a little "kissy-face" on the cheek. Within sixty seconds this guy will be excited!

The gal disappears and he quiets down. Lots of feelings are still present, though. In walks another girl and she does the same thing to him. Again, within sixty seconds this guy is excited. And then this gal disappears. This happens ten times in a row with ten different girls. And every girl gets him excited.

After I described this to the group of high schoolers, I asked, "What does this prove?" One sweet young thing in the front row piped up and said, "Mr. Poure, that proves he loves all ten!" After the laughter died down, I replied, "No, that only proves his machinery is working!"

The point is that love includes feelings, but you cannot depend on feelings to interpret love. Love is basically a commitment to another person. Jesus said, "Greater love hath no man than this, that a man lay down his life for his friends" (John 15:13 KJV). And the ultimate expression of Jesus' love was on a cross, where he died for you and me. Now, that is love! That is commitment!

The owner's manual tells us some other things about love. One of the greatest things your teens could do is to memorize the love chapter—1 Corinthians 13. Paul defines love here as "not selfish." The more perfectly you love, the more unselfish you become. We talked earlier about the root of sin being selfishness. And this can really create havoc in a marriage relationship. Young couples must struggle with this self-centered selfishness that keeps them from extending themselves to their spouse.

The basic motivation of love is objective, as opposed to subjective. This means that love gives. The more you love, the more you give. This self-giving love is characteristic of God's love for you and me. God loves us so much, "that while we were yet sinners (still rebelling and resisting), Christ died for us" (Romans 5:8 KJV). And you can't give more than your life.

Our struggle is compounded because there is a counterfeit for love. The counterfeit also has four letters—lust. And confusion arises because they both *feel* the same. For example, can a kiss be a sign of a genuine love? Of course. Can a kiss also be lustful? Certainly. Okay, what is the difference between a lustful kiss and a "love-full" kiss? Same pucker. Same vacuum. Even the same people. Confusing, isn't it!

This is usually a bigger problem for the girl than for the guy. She might be genuinely in love with the guy, and the guy might be genuinely in lust with her! You see the problem? And what makes it even more difficult is they both use the same words: "I love you." Often the guy will come along and add to these words something like: "Now you SAID that you love me, but tonight I want you to prove it." That's not love; that's lust.

I always told my daughter that if some guy moves out of line with her like that she should tell him point blank, "If you happen to be the guy I marry one day, I want to give myself completely to you, but until that day, will you please keep your cotton-pickin' fingers to yourself!" I've told groups of high school kids what I told my daughter, and usually one girl in the group comes up to me afterwards and says, "Mr. Poure, if I said that to my boyfriend, he'd get mad and take me home and never take me out again." And I shoot right back at her, "Girl, that's the best thing he could do! That would be wonderful! If that's the only reason he's taking you out, he's not in love with you, he's in lust with you." Of course, if that's what a girl wants from the relationship, there's little you can do or say. But if she wants more than that, she must understand the difference between love and lust.

Love is an objective force—looking out for the other person. Lust is a subjective emotion—centered around me. Bill Gothard says in his seminars, "True love can always wait to give.

But lust can never wait to get." I think that spells out the difference quite clearly.

I read in one of those advice columns in the newspaper recently about a guy who wrote in and asked, "What should I do? I've been living with two different girls in the same town, and somehow they found out and both dumped me. I'm so discouraged. Please don't give me any morality jazz, just a straight answer—what shall I do?" Well, sometimes these columnists miss it, but this one was right on target. The answer read, "Dear Discouraged: The basic difference between animals and humans is morality. And if you don't want any 'morality jazz,' go see your veterinarian!" This guy wasn't in love; he was in lust.

The trouble is that so much of this misleading information can take away from that beautiful intimacy that is possible in a marriage relationship. Lust can continue on into a marriage. Many times a wife will pick up the attitude or feeling that she is being used, that her husband is like an animal. When that happens, the husband is appealing to his wife on a lust level and not really loving her in kindness and understanding. He is not taking the time to be a lover because he can't wait to "get."

Now how do you help your kids find out what marriage is really all about? How can you help them marry in honor—marry in the Lord? To begin with, you need to have some good definitions. We've already worked out one for the difference between love and lust. How about marriage? How do you describe to your junior high schooler what marriage really involves? Well, don't be afraid to be profound, just don't be confusing. I think you can take a seventh grader and say something like, "Marriage is a blending or fusion of two individuals in such a way that they work and function as one unit; yet they both retain their own distinct identities." That may seem like a heavy definition, but kids can absorb that, especially if you take the time to talk through the points they don't understand.

A lot of young people never think this deeply about the marriage relationship. I've talked to guys and gals who say, "We're going to get married." I ask them, "Well, do you have any plans—have you really talked it through?" And they answer, "Oh, if it doesn't work out, we'll get a divorce." Even before they are married, these guys and gals are copping out. Their parents never really helped them understand the true meaning of marriage.

This attitude grows out of the widespread confusion over whether marriage is a private action of two persons in love or a public act of two people pledging a contract. The truth of the matter is that marriage is neither of these two. It is a covenant under God in the presence of fellow members of the Christian family. And this pledge is meant to endure, not because of the force of the law or the fear of its sanctions, but because of an unconditional covenant that has been made. A covenant goes way beyond a legal contract. We need to talk with our kids about these things. And the time to begin is when they start dating, if not before.

One of the key principles found in the owner's manual is that Christians are to marry *in the Lord.* We are not to be bound together with somebody who doesn't love the lord. (See 2 Corinthians 6:14.) Christians are to marry Christians.

Whenever I mention this to a group of kids, their first question is, "How about dating or going out?Do they all *have* to be Christians? I usually launch into a description of the five different degrees of boy/girl relationships. The first one is a *casual date.* That's a first-time date with someone. The second degree is the *friendship date.* Here you've been out with a person once and you've enjoyed their company, so you go out with them again. The third is the *steady date.* This usually involves a verbal agreement of exclusiveness to date only that one person. The fourth is *engagement* and the fifth is *marriage.*

With my kids, I said, "A casual date? No problem. If your life is bright and shiny, and you're alive for Jesus, don't worry about it. Just be free to go out with a person just because you want to." Whenever I've said this in a family seminar, someone always reacts by telling me, "I tell my children they are *never* to go out with anybody who isn't a Christian." But how do you find that out? A guy calls up and asks, "Hey, how about going to the football game with me tonight?" "Well," the young gal answers, "I must first ask you a question. Are you a Christian?" That's ridiculous—it just doesn't work that way. So I don't get restrictive here—within reason, of course.

What about friendship dating? I think even here it's possible that a friendship can be maintained between a Christian and a non-Christian. The Christian can maintain an effective witness, *if* his head's on straight. I just feel better being aggressive here and not defensive. So many parents say to their kids something like, "You can't go out with those people, you'll get sin-germs on your body." I get weary of that kind of argument. Christians are to be the salt in the world, and they are to wear the armor of God. Jude tells us we can even go into the gates of Hell to pluck out and rescue sinners. I believe that means we can encourage our kids to be positive and aggressive.

I remember one time when our son David was going to go out with a girl we didn't know. He willingly agreed when I suggested he stop by to introduce us to her before going out. And when she walked through that front door, I want to tell you, I was impressed with his taste! She was a doll! She had long flowing hair, beautiful eyes, and all the rest of her was gorgeous to match. She stood there clinging to David as he introduced us. "Hi, Mr. and Mrs. Poure," she said. I hardly heard her because I was praying,

"Lord, protect my son."

When David got home that night, we just happened to be awake. I walked into the kitchen, faking a yawn as I asked, "Hi, David. Have a good time?" "Yeah, Dad." "Hey," I continued, "I'm glad you brought Debbie by so we could meet her. By the way, is she a Christian?" "No, Dad," he answered, "she's a real little pagan."

When I got back to our room, I found Melba sitting up, and she was asking, "Is she . . . is she . . . is she?" "No, honey," I said meekly, "she isn't." Well, I tell you, we were in turmoil. Finally my wise little wife said, "Wait a minute. We're acting like typical parents. Instead, let's ask God for some positive move we can take." And with that we went to sleep.

Next morning at breakfast I said, "David, about last night . . . you know, about Debbie . . ." And I remember that he pulled his spoon out of his cereal and kind of froze there with milk dripping on the table as I continued. "Mom and I talked about your dating her, and we are going to be praying . . . in fact, we are going to pray *with* you that God will really use you as a positive witness to Debbie that she might see Christ in you."

He gobbled it up—both our idea and his cereal! That's what I mean when I say you can encourage your kids to be aggressive Christians. And it works. The rest of the story is that two months later he took Debbie to a Youth for Christ rally in Long Beach, and I happened to be the speaker. I tell you, it was exciting to see Debbie be the first one to publicly commit her life to Christ that night. David didn't even marry Debbie, but he had a lasting influence on her life. So if your kid has his or her head together with the Lord, friendship dates with non-Christians can be a real positive challenge.

But when it came to steady dating, our rule was: *Never* with a non-Christian. Now I know that, just because a person knows the Lord, that doesn't solve the problems. Christian girls can get pregnant by Christian guys before marriage. That happens. But boy, I'll tell you, when both people are Christians, there's a Problem Solver that lives in both their hearts, and that's a tremendous advantage these days!

At first, I really didn't like this idea of going steady. I told my daughter she couldn't go steady until she was sixteen. When she was fifteen, she was a song-girl at school and was just a little bubble of joy. And she had a multitude of boyfriends! There were guys coming in the front door and guys coming in the back door—all at the same time. And they would stand around checking each other out, while Sandra was on the phone talking to another guy. Finally, I said to her, "Go on over to the church and pick out a nice Christian boy and go steady with him. It is time to 'dump the herd'!" We changed one of our family "traditions" on the spot because going steady can be practical at times.

One other point to consider regarding marrying in honor is the idea of virginity. You really need to help your kids with this simply because you can't go with them and protect them on their dates. You are forced to give them freedom here. Therefore, you need to prepare them by talking with them about some of the problems that can arise.

Why does God say, "Marry in honor?" Paul wrote, "For God wants you to be holy and pure, and to keep clear of all sexual sin so that each of you will marry in holiness and honor" (I Thessalonians 4:3,4 TLB). The implication of the text is that we are to marry as a virgin. In other words, we are to maintain self-control because there is a right time to share ourselves sexually with another person. This is a positive program in God's system! If you can get your kids excited about God's positive program for marriage, it will cause them to want to wait. Waiting isn't easy for anyone—especially the average teen— unless he can see light at the end of the tunnel. And the parents' task is to provide that light.

Let's consider the "why." Why does God say to reserve sexual intercourse for marriage? I believe there are several practical reasons. First, there's the fact that sexual intercourse cannot be rightfully entered into outside of the circle of marriage for anyone without them experiencing guilt and fear. Even the non-Christian guy or girl cannot give away his or her virginity, go home, take a shower, get in bed and honestly say deep down inside, "I feel good about what I did tonight." No, it's usually more like this: "Oh, oh, why did I do it? Because I love him. I do, don't I? Hmmm, I must, because I did it." So the next time the two are out together, they have sexual intercourse simply to prove to *themselves* that they meant it the first time. I know that guilt can be rationalized and the conscience can be stifled. But that simply proves my point. If it were right and proper, a person wouldn't have to stifle his conscience or rationalize his guilt.

Second, there is the problem of unwanted pregnancy. Even with the pill and other contraceptives, this continues to be a growing problem. God can forgive and forget problems like this, but there are always scars left in the memory. We can't seem to forget.

Another practical reason to avoid sexual intercourse outside of marriage is the possibility of venereal disease. Here in the Los Angeles area it has become a real epidemic among people under 25 years of age. It is estimated that up to 72% of the birth defects in newborn babies are either the direct or indirect result of venereal disease. That's staggering!

But beyond all these practical reasons, I think there is an even better reason. I've been talking to groups of kids about this subject for a number of years now, and many of them come back to me and say, "Mr. Poure, remember your sex talk? Remember that one on 'Why wait 'till marriage?' Wow, the Lord really used that in my marriage! I am so glad I waited!" Kids need to know God wants them to reserve themselves exclusively for the one they're going to spend the rest of their life with. The best possible reason is the joy that comes from waiting for the right time to enjoy a sexual relationship with someone special without fear and without guilt.

The time for kids to make that commitment to the future is when they are cool, calm and collected. That's why, at our camp, we have a time when kids can dedicate their sexual life to the Lord and to His plan. If they have already blown it, we tell them to ask God for forgiveness, to dedicate their future to him and to reserve themselves for the big Night of Nights.

Once this commitment is made, the pressure is on! Our sexually oriented culture, with the heavy use of sex in advertising and the availability of pornographic materials, creates all kinds of problems for kids who are serious about their future. One of the things they need to understand is that men and women are not wired the same way. There is a basic difference between the sex drive of a woman and the sex drive of a man.

Most of a woman's sexuality begins in her head. If she is turned off there, her whole plant shuts down. But the man's machinery can start working regardless of how he feels. You put a picture of Mr. America in front of most women, and they will say something like, "Aw, isn't he cute." Appearance isn't enough for a woman. She is turned on by the totality of a relationship.

But you pull out a picture of some cute little gal, stretched out on a bearskin rug, wearing some clinging, revealing gown, and there isn't a guy around who couldn't flip a little switch somewhere in his frontal lobe. And within sixty seconds, his biological engines would be running. Men and women are different in more ways than appearance. They are aroused differently, and kids need to know this.

The other point they need to understand is that the sex drive is progressive. I use a thermometer to illustrate this point. Obviously, the higher you go on the thermometer, the hotter things get!

It all begins with seeing, walking and talking. Now these are very innocent and necessary activities. But we all know they can be sexually arousing at times. Nothing wrong with that—or any of this, really—it's just where things begin.

The first physical contact is usually holding hands. You remember the first time you did this, don't you? You were probably around the age of thirteen or fourteen. Even at that age, the male ego finds this to be tough. You know the feeling. The guy looks over and sees the girl's hand, and he thinks something like, "Well, what if I try to hold her hand and she pulls back?" And so he sweats it out for an hour or so and then says to himself, "One for the money, two for the show, three to make ready, and ... Wow!" Oh that can be an exciting moment! Especially when she

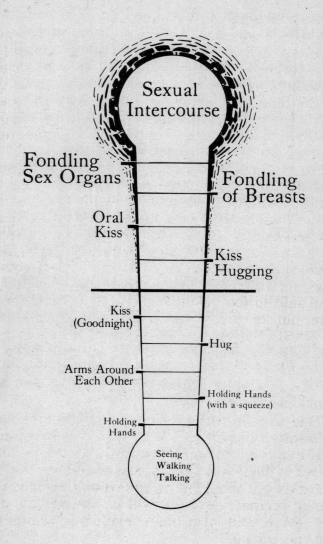

takes hold with a little squeeze!

That's all very mild, I know. But watch what happens. Soon both the guy and the girl accept it as a form of friendliness and it loses its thrill. Passion is progressive; so they have to move on up the thermometer to something more passionate. They move to a bigger "H." That's where you hold hands with lots of passionate squeezes. And soon that also loses its excitement value.

So the progression moves on higher and hotter. From holding hands, a couple moves to holding waists. And walking with your arms around each other is a bit more exciting than holding hands, especially for the guy. That's because his hands are wired. That's not something you learn in biology. You discover this fact from the owner's manual—the Bible. Paul said to the young women, "It is good for a man not to touch a woman" (I Corinthians 7:1 NAS). I'm sure Paul didn't mean some legalistic "no-touchy." What he refers to here is the sensual handling of a woman—it's harder for the guy to handle this than for the girl. So Paul says "Be careful."

This usually turns into a goodnight kiss and then into a bigger "K"—the kind of kiss where you hang on longer. I usually draw a line between these two kinds of kisses and say that is as far as you should go on your dates. Because if you go further, the body will be saying "go, go, go," when your previous commitment wants to say "no, no, no."

Kids will come up to me after a seminar and

ask, "How long can that little goodnight kiss last?" I answer, "Fifteen seconds, maximum!" I told one guy that and he countered with, "How many in a row?" If kids want to go past that point, I ask them why. And there's only one answer—it feels good. Believe me, I know it does and that's the problem. It feels so good that it just gets harder and harder to stop. Because the sex drive is progressive, the further you go the more intense it becomes. And soon you're out of control.

Some kids go on with their eyes open, knowing full-well what they are starting. They get into a make-out session which usually involves oral kissing, then some heavy petting which begins with the fondling of the breasts and the sex organs, and then ultimately right on into sexual intercourse.

You ask, "When should I tell my kids about this?" Well, I spell it out to junior highers at my seminars. Some of them just look at me and don't understand what I'm talking about. It doesn't bother them at all. But most of them understand! From the position of parental leadership, you need to explain this early.

When I talked with my son David about this, I started by asking him, "David, do you know the Bible says, 'Thou shalt not make out'?" He knew his Bible and that was a new one for him. So he asked, "Where's that verse, Dad? I've never read that before." So I showed him I Thessalonians 4:3 KJV, "You should abstain from fornication" and drew him a picture of the thermometer. When I drew the line, I said, "Everything above this line should be reserved for that one special gal in your life. It won't be easy to wait, but there is a right time for all of this." His eyes got big and he said, "When, Dad, when?"

It was a thrill to answer that question for him. I explained the marvelous system that God has developed for us to enjoy. All this passionate love play is part of His plan and is mandatory to prepare a husband and wife for the marvelous act of sexual intercourse.

I've talked with young couples who have told me they discussed the thermometer together when they started dating seriously. They wanted each other to know they had drawn a line. With that kind of communication and mutual commitment to the Lord, it was easier to reserve themselves for marriage.

When kids have dedicated their future to the Lord and committed themselves to stay pure for their future spouse, they will be willing to premeditate the pressure point and avoid temptation. I've talked with kids who have made this system work and they all have no regrets! You can't beat that kind of recommendation.

To Think About:

1. Write out a good definition of love and of marriage that you can share with your

children. Base your ideas on what you have read in this chapter, and adapt them to the ages of your kids.

2. What family traditions have you developed for your kids regarding dating? Do they understand the standards?

3. If you have children who are adolescents, sit down and discuss the thermometer with them. It is never too early or too late to talk together on this subject.

Chapter
9

A SPECIAL WORD
FOR THE KIDS

A Special Word
For The Kids

This chapter is for the kids. But I'm counting on your reading it first. Most of the directions in the owner's manual are aimed at the parents. But in the sixth chapter of Ephesians KJV, Paul begins by saying, "Children, obey your parents in the Lord: for this is right. Honor your father and mother; which is the first commandment with promise; that it may be well with you and that you may live long on the earth." Paul is not making a request here; he is stating a command—directed at children.

The interesting point here is the difference between honoring and obeying. Honoring goes beyond technical obedience. It is synonomous with obeying "in the Lord." Honoring is the *spirit* in which you obey. You can be obedient and not be honoring. A son is dishonoring while being obedient when he mows the lawn at his dad's request, but all the time he is mowing he is mumbling curses and threats against his dad. The lawn is mowed, but under protest. That is dishonoring.

Usually some kids come up to me after a session on this subject and say, "But Mr. Poure, you just don't know my parents. They don't deserve to be honored." I always remind them that this is a command. And the great thing is they don't have to trust their parents; they can trust God to lead them *through* their parents, whether they are Christians or not. And when kids do this, they often discover that their parents change in the process.

I had a young fellow come up to me at camp to talk about this. Earlier that day I had been talking to the group about honoring your parents and also about the authority the parent has over the child. This young man said, "Yeah, that's great for you to say, but my dad's not like you. When God said 'Honor your father,' He didn't know my dad! He's not fair!" "What do you mean," I asked. "How is he not fair?"

"Well, for example," he explained, "when I turned sixteen, he told me that I can use the car once a week if I have a legitimate use for it—like going on a date or something else important. But whenever I ask my dad for the car he says yes, but he always puts some dumb restriction on it."

"What kind of restriction," I asked. "He's like

a broken record," my young friend continued. "Every time he says, 'I want my car in my garage by eleven o'clock!' And that's not fair!"

"What's not fair about it?" I said as I pressed him for a reason. "Well, when I go to a game, it's not usually over until ten-thirty. Then I want to take my girl out to get something to eat, and then I have to take her home—and you can't do all that in thirty minutes!"

He had a good argument, but I pointed out, "Look, whose car is it?" "My dad's." So I said, "Okay, if your dad wants *his* car in *his* garage by eleven o'clock, what's not fair about that?" Then he got a funny look on his face and said, "When you say it, it doesn't sound unfair . . . But it *is* unfair!"

I asked him if he ever explained to his father why he needed an extra thirty minutes. "No," he told me, "I usually get so ticked off that I just grab the keys and go."

"That's where you're making a mistake," I said. Then I explained that he didn't have to agree with his parents, he just had to obey and honor them. "How," he asked.

So I set up a hypothetical situation for him. "Here's a suggestion for how you can handle it the next time. When your dad says, 'I want my car in my garage by eleven o'clock,' you say, 'Dad, before you make a final decision (and that phrase is priceless because you imply he hasn't made a final decision) let me explain . . . And here you explain three good reasons why you need the extra time. If your dad still doesn't agree, you say, 'Dad, I think I have given you three good reasons why I should be able to keep the car out until eleven-thirty, but if you say eleven, Dad, the car will be there.' " And then I suggested he add something like, "By the way, Dad, thanks for letting me use the car in the first place." And if he *really* wanted to get to his dad's heart, I told him to say something like, "And Dad, have a nice evening. Goodnight."

Now I had to warn him that he'd better spend some time praying in advance, asking that God would give him a real coolness of heart. But I also believed it would work wonders with his dad.

Several months later I got a letter from this fellow. I still have it, for it's a classic. At the top of the page are two words—"It worked!" And then the letter explained what happened. He told me that the next time he asked for the car, his dad came through with the exact same response. "But," he wrote, "Mr. Poure, you would have been so proud of me. I didn't lose my cool at all. I said exactly what you told me to say. And after I finished my explanation about why I should get an extra thirty minutes, my dad stood there and just played the same old record—'I want my car in my garage at eleven o'clock!' "

You could almost feel his excitement as he continued, "Mr. Poure, I was still cool. I said what you told me, and then I added, 'By the way,

Dad, thanks for letting me use the car in the first place. And have a good evening.' When I walked out of that house, my dad had a stunned look on his face. He looked like someone had just hit him on the head with a hammer.''

Then he continued with a description of the next weekend. When he asked for the keys, his dad said, "By the way, son, what time do you think you can have the car in the garage?" Isn't that neat? His dad was almost instantly changed when his son moved from simple obedience to honoring his father. And it works almost every time!

In wanting to make certain their kids do what they have been told to do, parents often clamp down on rules and neglect to listen. And adolescents, who are struggling to become their own person, too often try to establish their separate identity by a direct confrontation with their parents. This causes the parent to tighten the screws even further, which in turn creates more resentment and resistance in the young person. And soon you have a vicious cycle going that can destroy that family.

I've found that when children understand that honoring their parents is really the *attitude* in which they obey, they usually respond positively. At the same time, the children develop a good attitude towards authority as well. When this system is working, and the parent can sense this attitude in their children, they will give their kids more freedom. This is the path of progressive permissiveness that we talked of earlier. We can set in motion the cycle that makes the path smoother.

Since honoring parents is a commandment, children need to respond even when they don't feel like it. And as a result, they will discover a tremendous release that comes from the mutual trust that develops. It all boils down to attitude. In my travels, I've discovered that people are either praisers or groaners, and their attitudes have a tremendous effect on the other members of the family. Let's explore what it means to be a praiser.

To Think About:
1. Discuss with your family the difference between honoring and obeying. How do you define the difference in your own words?
2. Discuss with your children what they will be like when they are parents. How will they want *their* kids to respond to them?
3. Are there any areas in your relationship with kids in which you seem to have difficulty trusting them? Could you discuss with them your feelings on this?

Chapter
10

ARE YOU
A PRAISER
OR
A GROANER?

Are You A Praiser Or A Groaner?

If you could watch a rerun of your life for the past thirty days, what would you see? Are you a praiser or a groaner? Of course, the person who is a praiser is going to experience times of gloom and groans, for no one is perfect. But a praiser is a person who is walking under the influence of the Spirit of God on the sunny side of the street. The parent who knows how to praise God and praise his kids, in spite of the circumstances, creates a wholesome, healthy attitude within the family.

The interesting thing is this: The owner's manual—the Bible—commands each of us to be praisers! I discovered this while reading the Psalms. The Psalms are experientially oriented. They deal with life as it is, with all its ups and downs, tough times and happy times, and everything else that hits us in between. As I read through the Psalms, I found that the end of the book built into a kind of crescendo. There is a beautiful climactic finale that begins in Psalm 146 TLB. The first verse says, "Praise the Lord! Yes, really praise him!" Then the Psalm ends with the same words: "Praise the Lord!"

Psalm 147 TLB begins with the same theme: "Hallelujah! Yes, praise the Lord!" And all through this Psalm the theme continues to build. Psalm 148 instructs the heavens, the angels, the sun and moon and the stars to praise the Lord. Psalm 149 TLB repeats the refrain and then finishes with, "Hallelujah! Praise him!"

Finally, Psalm 150 TLB says:

> Hallelujah! Yes, praise the Lord!
> Praise Him in His Temple, and in the
>   heavens He made with mighty power.
> Praise Him for His mighty works.
> Praise His unequaled greatness.
> Praise Him with the trumpet and with lute
>   and harp.
> Praise Him with the tambourines and
>   processional.
> Praise Him with stringed instruments
>   and horns.
> Praise Him with the cymbals, yes, loud
>   clanging cymbals.
> Let everything alive give praises to the
>   Lord! You praise Him!
>   Hallelujah!

What a beautiful conclusion! And right there at the end, we are instructed to be praisers. If you are alive, you are to give praise. That's a command. If you choose to disregard the command, the option is to be a complainer and a groaner. And there are plenty of those folks around—we don't need anymore!

I wondered for a long time why God wants us to praise Him. If you were in one of my seminars, and I said to the group, "Everybody in the room is to praise me," you'd probably walk out. And as you left, you'd wonder what's wrong with Kenny Poure. Is his ego sagging? That's what I questioned about God. Why does He need all His little creatures to praise Him? The more I wondered, the more *good* reasons I came up with.

First of all, God wants us to praise Him because He knows that we are creatures of worship. If we don't praise and worship God, we will praise and worship someone or something else. But God just happens to be the only One in the universe who is worthy of consistent and continual praise. When God wants me to praise Him, it's not for His benefit; it's for my benefit. You see, praise is very healthy. When you praise God through worship, you are admitting to yourself that He is better than you are. And that forces you to get beyond yourself and focus in on the reality of God and His greatness.

Praise also keeps us in the center of God's will. The first article of the Westminster

Catechism says, "The chief end of man is to glorify God and to enjoy Him forever." For a long time, I wondered how I was to glorify God. Then I read in Psalm 50:23 KJV, "Whoso offereth praise glorifieth Me." Isn't that neat! So another reason to offer praise is that it glorifies God. Since this is God's will for me, it also satisfies my deepest needs.

Another practical reason for praise is that it prevents you from being a worrywart. You just can't praise the Lord and worry at the same time. It's impossible. I have found that praise is the one thing that gets me out of my depressed feeling quickly. It just dissolves away the blues.

I discovered this one morning when I was really down. The day before had been a real winner. It had been fantastically great. But this particular morning, I was really low. I got out of bed and said, "Lord, I haven't got time to be depressed—what are we going to do about it?" As I stumbled into the bathroom, I paused to look at myself in the mirror and said out loud, "Lord, help!" And I stood there looking at myself and thinking, "Well, Ken, guess it's just part of male menopause. When you hit the forties, you get depressed at times."

And the longer I stood there, the more depressed I became. I thought I'd better start jogging every day instead of every other day. Or maybe some extra push-ups would help. Then the thought came to me, "Let's do twenty-five 'Praise the Lords.' " I shut the door so Melba couldn't hear me and said, "Okay, here we go.

Praise the Lord, praise the Lord, praise the Lord
. . ." That's three. "Praise the Lord, praise the
Lord . . ." I got to ten and nothing happened. I
was as depressed as ever.

About that time a little voice in my head said,
"Poure, this is ridiculous. What are you doing?"
"Oh, I'm praising the Lord," I answered as I
started on number eleven. It took maybe two
more before I started to realize that I was
standing there praising the Lord God of
creation! He is the Alpha, the Omega, the
beginning and the end of everything. And then
all these thoughts started to gel in my mind as I
stood there praising the Lord. By the time I got to
twenty, I said, "Whew, praise the Lord!!" And
by twenty-five, I was out of the hole and ready to
face the day. It was fantastic!

A little later I read—again, in the owner's
manual—a verse that fit what I was doing. God
says in Isaiah 26:3 TLB that "He will keep in
perfect peace all those . . . whose thoughts turn
often to the Lord!"

The exciting thing about that promise is that
when my heart and mind are at peace, I am
much more sensitive to the needs of people
around me. You know how difficult it is to really
listen to the constant clamor of kids begging
for attention when you are all uptight.
"Mommy, Mommy, look at me. See what I can
do?" they seem to ask continually. The tense
mother says, "Later, can't you see how busy I
am worrying!" Well, she doesn't use exactly
those words; they are usually a little sharper.

You see, the attitude of praise towards God sets the pattern for my attitude towards my spouse and children. It becomes much easier to praise them for the neat little things they accomplish. Can you imagine what your family would be like if everyone around the house were a praiser? What a tremendous lubricant to family relationships!

For example, think how different this situation could be. A husband says, "Honey, would you iron my shirt while I finish getting dressed? I'm late and need to hurry." The wife snaps back, "How come you always wait until the last minute . . ." She certainly isn't practicing the attitude of praise. She's a groaner and complainer. The husband will get his shirt ironed, but there'll be a lot of tension before he leaves. The wife, in this situation, could possibly create the same tense atmosphere without saying a word. And obviously, the shoe could be on the other foot—the husband might imply by his attitude or statements that his wife is lazy; otherwise, his shirt would already be ironed. Praise is an action that is contagious. It very quickly infects our attitudes.

I remember vividly the day Melba grasped this concept. I'm a messy guy—I already confessed that to you. And when I leave the house in the morning, I leave a trail of chaos behind. Clothes are everywhere. My sweet little wife spent fifteen years trying to organize me and I have spent fifteen years resisting her efforts. "Pick up your clothes! And don't put the wet towel there! etc. etc." And I'd remind her, "My ministry is important! I don't have time for this!" And then she'd come back with, "How can we ever teach our children to be organized when their father is such a mess!" After fifteen years of that, you each become a pro at shutting out the other's groans and complaints. And she quit listening to my excuses.

One day I was walking out of the bedroom, and it was a disaster! I knew it. Melba was coming in as I was leaving; so I gave her a quick kiss and said good-by, hoping to avoid the sermon. As I walked on, I was waiting for at least one groan before I got to the door. But this particular morning I heard nothing—first time in fifteen years. In fact, I heard something I had never heard before. Melba was humming a little tune. That stopped me in my tracks—quick!

I quickly returned to the bedroom and carefully peeked around the corner of the doorway. There she was, picking up my mess and humming a tune. I was so curious, I startled her as I said, "Melba?" "Wha' Wha' . . . haven't you left?" she stammered in surprise. "No," I responded "What gives? What's with the humming and picking up my clothes and not saying anything to me? I mean . . ." "Oh," she said with such a sweet smile, "Will you forgive me?"

Well, now it was my turn to be startled. "For what?" I managed to ask. "For all these years I have complained, groaned and badgered you," she answered. She could tell I didn't understand. So she went on to tell me that the night before she had been reading her Bible and was struck by the fact that she was not a praiser. "And," she continued, "it broke my heart. I asked God to forgive me and now I'm asking you to forgive me."

Whew, I didn't know what else to say, so I said, "Yes, I forgive you" and ran on out the door. But you talk about power—there is power in an attitude of praise! That was fourteen years ago and I haven't missed a day since without picking up after myself.

You say, "I could be a better praiser if I didn't have so many problems." Or, "If only my kids weren't so hyperactive I could become a praiser." You know what? Problems are going to be with each of us until the day we die. We've all got problems. You get rid of two problems, and you discover five more. We've had three kids in our family, with the first one arriving when we were only eighteen-year-old kids. Now we have a new problem in our home—no kids. For what seemed like months, Melba walked around the house in a daze saying, "What do I do? What do I do?"

Problems change, but the command to be a praiser stays the same. And if it seems hard to praise God in the midst of turmoil, it seems to be even more difficult to take the time to praise our children. But one of the most powerful motivating forces for a child is the praise he receives from his parents. My philosophy on this is simple: When a child does well, you pat him on the back; and when he does wrong you pat him on the back—only a little farther down.

One of the most discouraging things a parent can do to a child, especially an adolescent, is to continually feed into his mind negative criticisms. If every message is critical, the child can't do anything to please the parents, and pretty soon, he doesn't care about much of anything. Then you've really got problems.

You see, I happen to know this is true. Praise is still important to me. I was reading a book written for women (I do that every so often, just to find out things about me) and the writer was talking about how husbands need praise. I didn't agree with her. She said, "Do you have a husband (written for wives, remember?) that sometimes walks into the bathroom while you're fixing your hair. He's in his shorts and he saunters in, strolls up to the mirror, flexes his muscles and says, 'Hey, take a look. Not bad, eh?' " And I'm thinking to myself, "Yeah, that's me. I do that sometimes."

But then this book went on to say, "Do you know why your husband does that? He's doing it because he's starving for your attention and your affection. Don't miss that clue." I shut the book and thought, "That's ridiculous! A forty-year-old man looking for attention? That's stupid! She doesn't know what she's talking about."

I was so bothered, I found the place and had Melba read it. She made a few "hummms" and simply said, "Interesting." And then we both got involved with something else.

Several weeks later, Melba was in the bathroom fixing her hair. I strutted in, threw a big flex on my biceps and asked, "How's that?" She turned around, looked carefully for a few moments and then said, "Wow, I don't know anyone as strong as you. That's just amazing!!" I blushed a bit and said, "Aw, it's not that great" and then walked out.

About an hour later it hit me. I suddenly realized what I had done. I yelled at Melba, "That book's right!" It seemed so silly when I read it, but the author was right on target. The need for praise is basic to each of us, regardless of our age. Not only should we be sensitive to our spouse's need, but we must take special care to satisfy the need for praise in our children as well.

Parents have all kinds of opportunities to praise their children. The problem is that we usually pay attention to our kids' negative behavior and take their good behavior for granted. I remember the time we were trying to teach our son David to take out the trash without being told every time. It was a painful ordeal to teach that kid *anything*. And this task was no exception. We tried everything. For weeks I would go into his room when he was asleep and try "sleep-teaching." While he lay there, I would repeat softly several times, "David, take out the garbage in the morning." It didn't work.

Then we tried pulling the trash box out from under the sink. But the kid was so blind he almost tripped over it several times. If he did see the box, he usually walked around it. Occasionally we would succeed and he would take the box out without being told.

One morning we spotted him going out the back door with the trash box in his hands. I said, "Melba, did you tell him to take out the trash?" "Not this morning," she answered. Amazing! He was doing it without being told. We were so excited, you'd think he'd just been named the Most Valuable Player in the Little League All-Star game. I had an idea. "Melba, let's be standing here by the door when he comes back in. Fold your arms and act like a parent. Let me do the talking."

As David walked back into the kitchen, he gave us a funny look—mostly because of the way we were standing. He gingerly walked over to the sink and put the empty box back in its place. I said, "DAVID?" "Yes," he answered, looking even more puzzled than before. "Do you know what you did this morning?" I asked. "No, Dad, what?" And with great pride in my voice, I said, "You took out the trash this morning without having to be told. Do you know what that tells us about you?" He shook his head from side to side. I continued, "That tells us you are growing up. You are becoming a responsible young man, and we are so proud of you!"

You could almost see his little ego expanding as he swaggered out of the kitchen with a very satisfied look on his face. You know what? For three whole days we didn't have to remind him to take out the trash!

Praise works! When we praise God, we change because our attention is directed at the only One worthy of worship. When our homes are filled with praise for each other, our families are strengthened because each member of the family feels worthy. Good, healthy self-esteem has a chance to grow and develop.

Praise provides the foundation for all the other things you as a parent can do to give your kids a chance. Put them all together and they will work miracles. And someday, your kids will rise up and call you blessed!

To Think About:
1. Which are you—a praiser or a groaner?
2. Look back over the past seven days. When did you praise the individual members of your family? For what?
3. Make a list of at least five things for which you could sincerely praise each member of your family today. Make a point to praise them for one of these things each day for the next five days. Now that you have the habit started, keep on being a praiser!